Disciple Building: Life Coaching

Meeting People Where They Are, Helping Them Take The Next Step®

BOB DUKES

Disciple Building: Life Coaching
(Version 2.15)

Worldwide Discipleship Association
(Attention: Margaret Garner)
P.O. Box 142437
Fayetteville, GA 30214 USA
E-mail: mgarner@disciplebuilding.org
Web Site: www.disciplebuilding.org

NOTE:
In an effort to recognize that both men and women are co-heirs of God's grace, we have chosen to use alternating gender pronouns in this document. However, we do recognize and embrace gender-specific roles in Scripture.

Development and Writing Team:
Bob Dukes (Primary Author)
Margaret Garner
Jack Larson
David Parfitt
Buddy Eades

Cover Design by Cristina van de Hoeve / DoodlingDesigner.com
Page Design and Layout by Cara Stein / BookCompletion.com

Table of Contents

Introduction

When I return to my hometown I often meet someone who says, "I'll never forget your dad. He taught me to play baseball." My Father coached in the recreation league for nearly twenty years. Several of his players played professionally, including two of my brothers. (Watching one of them pitch a scoreless inning in the World Series is still one of the highlights of my life.) Ironically "Pap" was never a star himself. Most of his short career was spent in the minor leagues during the Depression, struggling to find a place in the starting rotation. But he loved the game. He died several years ago but his legacy lives on, immortalized by a small plaque at one of the city parks and through the lives of countless boys who played on one of his teams.

He coached at a time when some fathers were unavailable, so he became a surrogate dad to my friends, instilling skills on the field and discipline in the dugout. But there was something else. After the games the team would sometimes show up at our house for a meal. He would move from player to player replaying the game as he rubbed heads and offered words of encouragement. My father never achieved what many would call success, working hard all his life with few tangible results. But when I bump into one of his former players, I'm amazed at the impact of his life.

Nearly everyone I know has had a similar experience. For some it was a teacher who influenced their lives, others followed the lead of a drama coach, for some a music instructor or close relative helped to shape their formative years. Many young people had a coach similar to my dad, someone who taught them more than game strategies and mechanics. These people who influence and strategically shape the lives of others can be called Life Coaches. The most successful instill more than training and discipline, they impart their very lives to others. Of course, the best Life Coach of all is a caring parent. Moses admonished the parents of Israel to teach the laws of God to their children as they went about the routines of life. It was in the course of ordinary activities that lives were changed.

As you read and use the Life Coaching Manual, you will learn what Life Coaching means for a disciple builder. You will first learn what a Life Coach is and how she participates in helping others grow to Christlikeness. In addition to learning about your role, you will learn skills that will help you create a discipleship plan for individuals and groups. You will be able to use tools such as the *R-CAPS Grid* and the *Needs, Goals, Projects* Approach to help people take the next step to maturity both spiritually and practically, addressing needs that help individuals heal from emotional pain and also develop Christlike character. You will look at the ministry and person of Jesus and help people grow in a pattern based on His discipleship model. As you begin this journey, you will find that your ministry to others is much broader than merely communicating content, but involves developing a close relationship with another person. We believe the end result is that each person we coach will one day grow to model these same actions and recognize the value of investing in another person as well. As Paul first discipled Timothy, he saw Timothy take the things that were taught to him and practiced with him and in turn teach others who also would become disciple builders and Life Coaches. We at WDA believe that this manual will help you be more effective and fruitful in your ministry to others.

What Is A Life Coach?

It's uncertain exactly how the term "Life Coach" became part of the popular vernacular, but the concept describes a person who is able to provide guidance, insight, and experience to others who are striving to succeed at various endeavors. Used in the business world it refers to someone able to help others become profitable in commercial ventures. In athletics, it's a person who prescribes workout routines to maximize physical strength and prowess. Used in a more general sense, it means anyone skilled at helping others remain focused and goal-driven. Sometimes a Life Coach can be someone the 'disciple' has never actually met face-to-face. In these cases, the insights are gleaned from books and tapes or by attending conferences.

But this manual is about a different kind of Life Coach. It's about Christian leaders who are willing to invest their knowledge and experience and even their very lives so that others might learn to think, feel and act like Jesus. A spiritual Life Coach is a person who, in the midst of a caring relationship, imparts truth that changes the life (conduct/character) of another, gradually helping the disciple become more like Jesus Christ. In WDA, we often use the phrase, *"meeting people where they are, helping them take the next step®"* to describe the Life Coaching process. Those who are helped may not fully realize it until later, but they're forever impacted by the life and example of these leaders. It was Jesus who said "but

everyone [disciple], after he has been fully trained, will be like his teacher."(NAS) Used in this way, there's another term that can be substituted for "Life Coaching," "disciple building."[1]

Spiritual Life Coaching

Jesus Christ was the ultimate Life Coach. In the Gospel of John, He offers this promise: "The thief comes only to steal and kill and destroy; I came that they may have life, and have it abundantly." (NAS) The Great Commission given to His disciples in Matthew 28:18-20 is both a command and invitation to join Him on one of the greatest adventures in life: building disciples. Spiritual Life Coaching involves "teaching them to observe all that I commanded you."(NAS) There are two implications to this command that often escape our notice. The first is that the teaching should be comprehensive. We are to teach **everything**, not just the familiar principles or the introductory concepts. Spiritual Life Coaches must ask the question: "Is my coaching part of a larger, comprehensive plan to teach the whole curriculum of Christ?"

The second implication is that we should help the people we are teaching to actually **obey the truth**. I like to call this *doing* truth versus just *knowing* truth. There is a clear biblical priority to evangelize the nations and plant churches, but we must not forget that the Great Commission includes helping Christ's followers become "conformed to the likeness of His Son [Christ]." Our spiritual Life Coaching must be *intensive* and *intentional* enough to transform lives.

---

[1] We will be using several different terms interchangeably to describe Life Coaching as it relates to disciple building. (E.g. "spiritual Life Coach," "one-to-one disciple building," "discipler/disciple builder," etc.)

But any parent can tell you this is easier said than done. Teaching others to 'do' truth is a complex process that involves the changing of motives, values, and worldview. It also hopes to develop a walk of faith, teaching people how to trust God. This type of training cannot be accomplished in a classroom alone. It must be worked out in the context of real life experiences. Some of the concepts, such as how to develop and demonstrate mature love, are not simple. This is why spiritual Life Coaches are critical to the process. It's only in the context of a close relationship (where there is encouragement, accountability, prayer, and teaching) that this type of transformation can effectively occur.

The importance of the example and teaching of a spiritual Life Coach cannot be overstated. Paul admonished Timothy to follow him as he followed Christ. In another place the instruction was for Timothy to follow the "pattern of sound teaching" that Paul had taught. Timothy learned these truths from Paul in the context of close relationships. II Timothy 2:2 states, "The things which you have heard from me in the presence of many witnesses, entrust these to faithful men who will be able to teach others also." (NAS) Jesus, after washing His disciples feet as a model of Christian love and leadership, urged them, "Now that you *know* these things, you will be blessed if you *do* them" (emphasis mine).

We who build disciples should be encouraged by the importance God places on the Life Coaching process. The Scriptures remind us that anyone who aspires to the office of overseer has an honorable, noble role in the Kingdom. But we should also be sobered by the responsible role God expects us to play. Paul warns the Corinthian church that "each one should be careful how he builds. For no one can lay any foundation other than the one already laid, which is Jesus Christ." Paul goes on to explain that we can either build by using temporal materials or eternal materials, but there will be a Day when we must give an account for our work of building up others.

In order to be effective disciple builders, we must

> Our spiritual Life Coaching must be intensive and intentional enough to transform lives.

realize that God is the author and finisher of the process of sanctification. Paul states, "I planted, Apollos watered, but God was causing the growth." (NAS) In another place Paul asserts that "He who began a good work in you will perfect [complete] it until the Day of Christ Jesus." (NAS) Spiritual Life Coaches can take heart that God will sovereignly oversee the process.

The role of spiritual Life Coaching is only one part of the disciple building process. For years there has been a debate in disciple building circles about what is the best forum for helping people grow spiritually. The advocates of **small groups** can list examples of people whose lives have been changed by the intimacy and accountability of this arrangement, while the proponents of **one-to-one** discipleship (Life Coaching) cite the advantages of this format. Others extol the merits of **teaching and preaching,** or the benefits of being well-read. Some point out the importance of putting disciples into **ministry situations** as the best way to facilitate growth and development. The **spiritual disciplines** such as fasting, solitude, or personal devotions are mentioned by many as being especially beneficial in spiritual formation.

All of these forms constitute healthy approaches to spiritual development. All should be included as part of a disciple building program. Each format has certain advantages and certain limitations. It is valuable to note that Jesus used *all* of these forms as part of His disciple building training. Because the local church has all of these structures (e.g. small groups, teaching, preaching, etc.), it is the best location for making and training disciples if the structures are utilized strategically. Within the church there is a unique role for a well-equipped Life Coach. This person is able to "meet people where they are, and help them take the next step."

If disciple building is the overall process in which more mature believers assist less mature believers as they grow, then spiritual Life Coaching is the "one-to-one" part of the process. A Life Coach is able to help a disciple integrate and incorporate all the other growth processes into a unified whole. The Life Coach is responsible for tracking and overseeing the progress of the individual believers entrusted to his care. This individual encouragement and accountability is invaluable. As we will see later, this is best accomplished when the Life Coach works in concert with a team of others in a ministry context. One of the purposes of this manual is to offer assistance and coaching skills to help make the task of Life Coaching more manageable and successful.

Balancing Process And Programs, Mystery And Methods

One of my favorite destinations is The Cotswolds of England. Linda and I discovered this delightful part of the United Kingdom quite by accident. I was speaking at a forum near Oxford one summer and a friend suggested we take a driving tour through the surrounding countryside. Every turn of the road afforded new vistas of quaint villages constructed with the honey-colored stone that makes the region so famous. But the highlight for me was exploring the beautiful gardens of the area. Each was unique, but the most exquisite had one trait in common: they had been meticulously planned, planted, and nurtured by a master gardener.

In a similar way God has created each of us as individuals, uniquely designed to reflect His image and character. But He has created common growth patterns and processes that define and shape our development. This presents an interesting challenge and opportunity for a spiritual Life Coach. We need to understand the growth processes that God has established, and at the same time we must resist the notion that we can program growth. Not only is it impossible to program such complexity, it would be wrong to attempt it. God delights in the diversity and

uniqueness of the various parts of His creation, and man is His crowning creative achievement. The Fall has corrupted and tarnished mankind, yet sin has not completely obliterated His image in us. Disciple building is one of the means by which we are significantly restored to His image and to the purpose for which He created us.

Even though we are all uniquely created, this does not mean that we can't develop strategies to help each other grow. The objective is to understand and utilize the processes of spiritual growth while allowing room for the uniqueness of the individual and the (often) mysterious purposes of God. Jesus was the Master of living in the tension of mystery and method. While emphasizing the sovereignty and mystery associated with the working of God's Spirit in John 3:8, He also spoke of a discipleship training process in Luke 6:40. A careful study of the Gospels reveals that our Lord had an overarching strategy for developing His ministry and training His disciples. He repeatedly utilized five Life Coaching initiatives to prompt spiritual development in His followers. (We will learn more about these later.) In the midst of this coaching paradigm there was diversity and creativity.[2]

We All Need Encouragement.

I must confess that when I first typed the heading for this section I felt a little embarrassed, and somewhat irritated. My lingering false sense of masculinity still recoils from the idea of needing anyone to "come alongside and help." Growing up, I was intrigued by John Wayne and the ruggedness of the "loner" roles he played in the movies. This isolated approach felt "right" to me because I had been deeply wounded (emotionally) during my childhood, and one of my coping mechanisms was to withdraw from anyone who might get close enough to hurt me again.

But I'm learning that in order to heal, I need to get close to others. Being married to a wonderful friend has convinced me of the importance of intimate companionship. But every man needs another man who can confirm and validate him, and every woman needs another woman with whom to relate and com-

---

[2] On one occasion Jesus fed 5000 with five loaves and two fish. Another time He fed 4000 using a different combination. Once He healed a blind man by spitting in the dirt and applying a mud-poultice to his eyes. Another time He simply spoke and someone received sight. God meets each of us where we are, then He helps us to take the next step.

municate the deep places of her heart. There is an intimacy in relating to those of the same gender that opposite-gender love cannot achieve. Every TV commercial that focuses on the oddities of being "a guy with other guys" taps into this dynamic.

The trouble is that there are so few people who are 'safe' enough or accessible enough to approach. (But, here's the encouraging news: you wouldn't be reading this unless you were willing to expand these ranks!) Some who read this have never been "Life Coached" (discipled) themselves. Others may have some experience in helping others grow. This manual is designed to help anyone who wants to learn more. Regardless of your experience, I hope you can pick up new ideas that will make you even more effective. The learning curve may be steep and the obstacles myriad, but the benefits far outweigh the liabilities. I hope you will continue and never stop learning. The health and welfare of the family, the church, and society depends on people like you who aspire to help others grow to maturity.

> The health and welfare of the family, the church, and society depends on people like you who aspire to help others grow to maturity.

We Have a Partnership with God.

Spiritual transformation is accomplished partly through a unique partnership between God and individual Life Coaches He appoints to assist Him in the proclamation of truth. Paul explains this dynamic in I Corinthians when he says that he planted and Apollos watered but it was God who was causing the growth. It is important to note that there are distinct stages of growth mentioned. Paul was used by God at the initial stage of planting the seed of Christian truth leading to conversion, then Apollos came afterward to help the truth take root and continue to grow. Later we will explore in more detail some of the progressive stages of spiritual growth. By understanding this progression, a Life Coach is better equipped to help others.

Scripture is filled with admonitions that leaders in the church should help younger believers grow and develop. But this begs the question: "How do we help someone else grow?" As already stated, we should resist the idea that spiritual development can be reduced to a program, but wise Life Coaches can design and implement specific growth projects that meet individual disciples at their point of need and help them take the next step in their development. Though there aren't formulas for growth, there are growth initiatives that Life Coaches can utilize to help others progress in their faith development.

The Five Initiatives Of A Life Coach

I have a friend who knows my penchant for metaphysics, biblical theory, and systematic theology and keeps me honest by always asking the practical questions. It's not that he's opposed to the philosophical, he simply wants to know: "Does it WORK in real life?"

Let's face it, unless Life Coaching works in the fast-paced world where most of us reside, it's of little use. But Jesus made it work in His world, and without all the "bells and whistles" of modern technology to assist Him. This begs the question: What did our Lord actually DO to disciple The Twelve? In other words, if Jesus had a day-planner, what Life Coach activities or initiatives would He have scheduled?

A careful study of Scripture gives us clues into how biblical "Life Coaches" facilitated the process of helping others grow. In effect, they engage in five activities or initiatives of disciple building:

[1] they build *Relationships*,

[2] they teach *Content*,

[3] they provide *Accountability*,

[4] they *Pray*, and

[5] they construct *Situations* where truth can be applied.

These five initiatives form an acrostic: R-CAPS. When combined with an understanding of the phases of progressive growth, these five initiatives form a disciple building training/growth grid.[3] The

---

[3] See *R-CAPS Grid* on page 54.

R-CAPS approach has been helpful to many as a guide for assisting Life Coaches in the growth process. *R-CAPS* is not a curriculum or a program, but a framework for understanding what disciple builders can actually do to help others grow. Let's take a closer look at each of these five initiatives.

Build Relationships

Paul said to the Thessalonian church that he and the other members of his team were like fathers and mothers, caring, nurturing and teaching the believers (I Thessalonians 2:7-12). The relationships that they established provided the foundation for everything else that God was doing. Generally, the impact someone has upon us is in direct proportion to the relationship we have with that person. Casual acquaintances may irritate us with their comments or actions, but not to the same degree as remarks made by people we know well.

Close relationships can be painful as anyone who has been emotionally hurt can readily attest. But they can also be wonderful and helpful. A compliment from a trusted friend carries more weight than a flattering remark made by a stranger. The trusted family physician is able to diagnose problems before they become life-threatening because we allow the doctor to 'probe and poke' us in very personal ways. In a similar way, a Life Coach is able to keep watch over a disciple's soul. For the process to be effective, a safe relationship must be established.

Safe relationships require time, shared experiences, and honest communication. Stephen Covey

asserted that relationships are a lot like bank accounts. In a relationship with a banking institution we make deposits and then make withdrawals. The account is active and healthy as long as we make enough deposits to offset our withdrawals. In the event we overdraw the account, the bank informs us and penalties are assessed. If we continue to operate the account at a deficit the account will eventually be closed.

Many marriages begin with a large relational account balance. Courtships are times when both the man and the woman strive to convince the other of their love and loyalty. These same couples will often conceal their relational shortcomings. But after the wedding, real-life happens and weaknesses are revealed. Instead of continuing to make emotional "deposits," the couple begin making "withdrawals." Sometimes the result is divorce. But most often the couples who work hard at maintaining good communication and servicing the relationship enjoy many wonderful years of marriage.

Similarly, for the Life Coach relationship to be effective, a Life Coach must make emotional deposits in order to establish trust. This is important because at some point the disciple builder may have to make strategic emotional withdrawals. Whenever we confront someone about an area of inconsistency or disobedience, we run the risk of encountering defensiveness, jeopardizing the relationship. Unless a Life Coach can point out areas where growth needs to occur, the growth process breaks down.

The goal of Life Coaching is: *to encourage growth in Christlikeness by the application of truth in* **the context of the loving accountability of a trust relationship.** Key words are "loving," "accountability," and "trust." Love is a dominant theme throughout Scripture. Your one-to-one Life Coaching relationships must be motivated by and infused with genuine agape love. Accountability must be voluntary; accountability achieved under pressure or by demand will lead to resistance and legalism. To have an effective disciple building relationship, trust must be *given* to the Life Coach by the disciple—not demanded or assumed.

The Importance of Trust

As Life Coaches, we can proclaim the authority of the Bible and can appeal to and advise disciples based on that authority. However, for trust and accountability to be given completely and voluntarily, a healthy relationship between the Life Coach and disciple must be established. Some trust is achieved by virtue of position. However, real, lasting trust that fosters openness and vulnerability can *only* be built through an ongoing relationship where life experiences and hearts are shared. Thus, it is important that you as a Life Coach not force trust, but instead develop your personal relationship with the disciple in a manner that encourages trust to be given.

An attitude of humility toward the disciple is essential in developing trust and accountability. Humility can show itself in two ways. First, you as the Life Coach should make every effort to be open and vulnerable with your disciple. Share your struggles and failures; be real about disappointments and shortcomings. This obviously needs to be done wisely and with discernment since acknowledging that you have problems and allowing your disciple to watch you deal with them does much to encourage trust.

Second, humility is demonstrated when a disciple builder has the attitude of working with the disciple on areas of growth. Instead of having the "I will help you grow" mentality, trust is built when the disciple builder has the "Let's help each other grow" mentality. Although the Life Coach is the leader in the relationship, the disciple building relationship should never be a one-way street with the Life Coach doing all the giving. It is a two-way street, and this attitude needs to be communicated to the disciple in word and deed.

Other Relational Character Qualities of a Life Coach

Obviously, all of us—Life Coaches and disciples alike—should be growing in Christlikeness. Along with love, accountability and trust, there are four other important qualities in the life of the Life Coach that facilitate relationships: security in God, discretion, ability to keep a confidence, and flexibility.

Being secure in your personal relationship with

God is crucial for being a successful Life Coach. The Life Coach who is insecure may want to be liked or approved of by the disciple to such an extent that she loses her boldness and directness when difficult issues arise. By contrast, a secure Life Coach is able to encourage, rebuke, teach and correct as God leads regardless of the response of the disciple. In actuality, much of contemporary ministry is what many counselors refer to as 'caretaking.' Caretaking describes the situation that develops when a Life Coach is more concerned with getting her own needs met than with meeting the needs of the disciple. The root of caretaking is insecurity.

Discretion and the ability to keep a confidence also help build a trusting relationship. Discretion means showing good judgment in your conduct, especially your speech. This implies that you are cautious in what you do and say and consider the effect your example has on others. Keeping a confidence involves not telling others specific information about the relationship. On the positive side, keeping confidences protects the integrity and confidentiality of the disciple. A disciple should know with certainty that the Life Coach will be careful not to even allude to any private information in conversation with others. We in the disciple building trade refer to this as being a 'safe' person. Becoming a safe person is one of the most important priorities for the Life Coach. Jack Larson, Director of WDA's Restorative Ministry, lists some of the characteristics of safe people:

- They listen well, make eye contact and offer advice only when appropriate.

- They communicate understanding whenever possible.

- They allow the disciple to 'be himself.'

- They are sympathetic.

- They validate the feelings of those who speak to them.

- They maintain confidentiality.

- They refrain from judging or rejecting the disciple.

Finally, flexibility is absolutely essential as you build a relationship with your disciple. As the Life Coach you make plans for your time together, and most of the time the plans can be carried out. However, you must be sensitive to changes that need to be made and be willing and able to make them. Your ability to do this smoothly and with discernment will increase with experience and personal growth.

Modeling in Relationships

Paul told Timothy to follow him as he followed Christ, underscoring the priority of leading by example. My dad taught my brother to throw a curveball and a change-up by demonstrating the techniques firsthand. A good Life Coach says, "Watch me!" Modeling the Christian life is perhaps the most powerful and beneficial ingredient in the process of relational Life Coaching.

At a recent gathering of WDA alumni I was approached by one of the men that I had discipled years before. He told me how much he appreciated the time and effort I had put into preparing the studies and lesson plans for our small group and personal appointments. But then he added, "Truthfully, I really can't remember many of your Bible studies. I'm sure they were interesting, but what I remember most is you and Linda opening your home every Saturday morning and cooking breakfast. You also invited us to drop in after ball games in the evening and stay into the wee hours of the morning. You allowed us to be a part of your family. Now that I'm married, I realize that those hours we spent together formed the foundation for my own home. The relationship gave me a context and motivation for listening to what you taught."

Did you get that last point? The receptivity to truth was an extension of the relationship. We see this evidenced in the Scriptures after Jesus delivered a blistering sermon regarding priorities. The text in John 6 reports that many of His disciples "turned back and no longer followed Him." Turning to the original disciples who had been with Him since the beginning, He asked, "You do not want to leave too, do you?" Peter, the self-appointed spokesman for the group, replied, "Lord, to whom shall we go? You have the words of eternal life. We believe that You are the Holy One of God."

The relationship Jesus had established with His disciples provided the resiliency for them to remain with Him even when the truth was difficult to embrace. And because they remained with Him, they eventually understood that His words and teachings were indeed eternal and worth following, showing that He was the Lord and King. If we build solid relationships, we can say hard things and expect our words to affect life changes.

Teach Content

An effective spiritual Life Coach must also be able to teach the content (truth) of the Kingdom and help the disciple apply it. The Great Commission exhorts us to "go and make disciples of all nations," and then teach these disciples "to obey everything I [Christ] have commanded." Paul reminded young Timothy to entrust the biblical truth he'd been taught to "faithful men who will be able to teach others also."(NAS) Paul emphasized the priority and power behind this exhortation by saying, "All Scripture is inspired by God and profitable for teaching, for reproof, for correction, for training in righteousness, so that the man of God may be adequate, equipped for every good work." (II Timothy 3:16-17, NAS)

Transmitting biblical content is at the heart of building disciples. Specialized research and training can be valuable in this endeavor, but teaching others doesn't require a seminary degree. There are many excellent study aids and resources available for lay Life Coaches to be able to teach effectively. But teaching others does require diligence and study. Paul urged Timothy to study to show himself approved, as a workman who handles the word of truth accurately. There's no substitute or shortcut for disciplined study.

But God helps us as we help others understand the Scriptures. He gives us insight and understanding to teach, and the Holy Spirit is at work helping the disciple to deepen his understanding and apply the truth. Jesus said, "If you hold to my teaching, you are really my disciples. Then you will know the truth,

and the truth will set you free." (John 8:31-32) Content is more than informational, it's transformational.

Being emotionally "set free" is vital to spiritual growth. In John 10:10, Jesus described Satan as a thief who comes to steal, kill, and destroy. Other passages make it clear that a primary weapon of the evil one is a system of lies. These lies are powerful because they're so believable, often transmitted in the midst of painful, emotionally-charged situations. They wound us deeply, making it very difficult to believe the truth.

Taking Thoughts Captive

A primary role of a Life Coach is to help a disciple recognize the lies of the evil one and use the truth of God's Word to offset the falsehood. This type of teaching must be more than instructive, it must also provide encouragement and edification (cf. Hebrews 3:12-13). In a letter to the Corinthian church, the Apostle Paul explains that there is a type of spiritual warfare that involves pulling down strongholds (of unbelief) and *"taking every thought captive"* (emphasis mine) (II Corinthians 10:5, NAS) to the obedience of Christ. Biblical truth/content offsets the lies of the enemy as it's delivered by a Life Coach who sincerely cares.

The truths about God are often written in the form of specific promises about the relationship God desires to have with His people. Paul reports that these promises have been secured by and fulfilled in the person of Jesus Christ, and they are all reserved for the believer. Peter confirms this, stating in his second letter that the promises of God are "precious and magnificent" (NAS), and they are the basis for us to "participate in the divine nature, having escaped the corruption in the world." Later he adds that we should apply them by making "every effort to add to your faith, goodness; and to goodness, knowledge," etc. This passage goes on to explain that as we grow in our knowledge and understanding of Christ, we grow in our capacity to love Him and one another.

In Colossians 1:28-29 Paul reminds his readers that his mission was to proclaim Christ and admonish and teach everyone with all wisdom so that he might present everyone perfect (mature) in Christ.

(Here again we see the link between teaching truth and the process of conforming the disciples to the character of Christ.) But Paul insists that this must be done "with all wisdom" to be effective. In another place Paul refers to a "pattern of sound teaching" and actually admonishes Timothy to guard the good deposit entrusted to him, and then to entrust the same truths to reliable men who will also be qualified to teach others (II Timothy 1:13-2:2).

This "pattern of sound teaching" that Paul mentioned is nothing less than the same content or teaching that the first apostles were commissioned to teach the disciples who followed Christ (Matthew 28:18-20). But the content was to be put into practice or obeyed. This teaching involved more than the communication of information. It was truth that was to transform the lives of the hearers. As we have seen, some of the power to transform was in the very truth itself. But implicit in the commission to teach is the responsibility of the leader to see that the truth was applied, or put into practice. This is the focus of much of the Book of James which insists that we become not merely people who listen to truth (hearers), but we become people who apply the truth (doers) (James 1:22).

The role of the Life Coach is to teach truth so that the disciple is able to **do** the truth. WDA has developed resources and training to help the Life Coach know what to teach the disciple and how to help the disciple apply it. Included in Exhibit A on page 47 of this manual are five charts entitled *What Jesus Did/What We Can Do* which list Scripture references in the Gospels of what Jesus taught His disciples. Also, WDA has developed the *Christian Growth Checklist (CGC)* that outlines many of the strategic content objectives for each phase of the growth process. We have also designed a series of Pocket Principles®, Teaching Outlines, and Guided Discussions that provide these theological concepts in varying formats for each of the progressive phases of spiritual growth. These resources are part of an ex-

> The role of the Life Coach is to teach truth so that the disciple is able to *do* the truth.

tensive curriculum that is designed to help a Life Coach teach everything that Jesus commanded.[4]

Provide **A**ccountability

The role of teaching content can engender images of classroom instruction. There's certainly a place for this type of teaching but, as we have already seen, the teaching role of the Life Coach is more dynamic. Applying truth also involves holding people accountable to act on what they know. The writer of Hebrews gives us a clue about the importance of accountability when he says, "See to it, brothers, that none of you has a sinful, unbelieving heart that turns away from the living God. But encourage one another daily, as long as it is called Today, so that none of you may be hardened by sin's deceitfulness." Later he says, "Let us consider how we may spur one another on toward love and good deeds. Let us not give up meeting together, as some are in the habit of doing, but let us encourage one another." (Hebrews 3:12-13, 10:23-25) The point is clear: we need to be encouraged (exhorted) to obey the truth and to turn away from sin and disobedience. The act of "spurring one another on" (or holding people accountable) toward Christlikeness is a key component of Life Coaching.

The task of motivating someone else to grow is a complex one and at the heart of what it means to be a disciple building Life Coach. Truth needs to be internalized to become real in our experience, and to become internalized we must be willing to obey truth even when it doesn't feel truthful or helpful. For this to effectively occur, the Life Coach must sometimes hold the disciple accountable to put truth into practice. Loving accountability in the Life Coach relationship is therefore paramount.

But accountability involves more than simply demanding obedience to truth. Real accountability does not force truth upon a disciple, and it certainly does not use the Life Coach relationship to coerce the disciple to behave in a particular way. Legalism can

---

[4] http://www.disciplebuilding.org/store

cause serious damage to spiritual development. There is a process of discipline and correction that exists in Scripture (Matthew 18:15-16; Galatians 6:1-2; Titus 3:10). We are urged to enter this process with restoration and healing as the ultimate goal. Unfortunately, there has been much spiritual abuse in the name of accountability.

Misunderstanding how to help someone put truth into practice has caused some people to mistrust the process of disciple building altogether. This is unfortunate, but understandable. Biblical disciple building should be characterized by agape love which is patient, kind, and humble. The wise Life Coach will keep the following principles foremost as he strives to encourage his disciple to grow by putting truth into practice.

Accountability should be: an extension of a caring relationship, linked to maturity, and not an end in itself.

1) Accountability Should Be an Extension of a Caring Relationship.

We mentioned earlier the importance of loving relationships in disciple building. If your disciple likes you and trusts you, she will be more open to your exhortation, and if you genuinely care, you will be more likely to challenge her appropriately.

2) Accountability Should Be Linked to Maturity.

Accountability needs to be linked to the appropriate level of maturity. The illustration of raising children helps us understand the importance of this maturation factor. There are certain directives, such as driving the family automobile on an errand, that a parent may appropriately give a teenager, but which would be totally inappropriate for a child of three. Conversely, it is not that unusual for a three-year-old to throw a temper tantrum, but if a teenager behaves in this way, we are shocked. The way discipline and incentives are meted out in a family depends on the age of the child.

Unlike physical growth, chronological age is not the defining point for spiritual maturity. Obedience to truth, evidenced by character and conduct, is the marker of maturity. The writer of the Book of Hebrews says that he was unable to teach certain content about God because the readers had not applied the truth they had already received. He lamented that at that particular point in their spiritual journey they should have been further along on the growth continuum. But instead of being mature, they were still spiritual infants. There are truths that correspond to specific levels of spiritual maturity, and these truths can only be applied at that point of maturity (Hebrews 5:7–6:3).

To hold someone accountable to obey a truth that is "outside the envelope" of their phase of growth can lead to frustration and discouragement. Conversely, to **not** hold someone accountable to obey truth that is appropriate can lead to stagnation and a withholding of vital nutrients for further growth. This may have been what Paul meant when he urged Philemon, someone who was gifted and skilled in ministry, to "be active in sharing your faith, so that you will have a full understanding of every good thing we have in Christ." (v.6)

3) Accountability is Not an End in Itself.

To be most effective, accountability should be linked to an overarching project of spiritual development. In the book *How People Grow*, Drs. Cloud and Townsend say that "accountability is very important, and the Bible tells us over and over again to build it into our lives. But here is the caution: *accountability is not a cure for lack of self-control.* The problem with accountability is that all that it does is count. It is like the temperature gauge on a car; it can tell you the engine has problems, but it can't fix it. A *person with a problem has to enter the process of discipline and structure....*"[5] This process of discipline and structure is called disciple building.

In a later section we will explain more about how

> Accountability should be an extension of a caring relationship, linked to maturity, and not an end in itself.

---

[5] Dr. Henry Cloud and Dr. John Townsend, *How People Grow* (Grand Rapids, MI: Zondervan, 2001), 126.

to design an overarching project that meets the disciple at the specific point of his maturity and also holds him accountable to take the next appropriate step. This strategic approach to accountability is more than asking people, "Are you doing certain things or not doing certain things?" It involves helping them refocus themselves on an overall approach to living the Christian life that gives them encouragement and perspective, even if they temporarily fail in the attempt. The first approach can lead to guilt and shame that short-circuits growth. The second leads to hope and a recommitment to maturity.

Pray

I have always believed in the power of prayer. (What self-respecting Christian leader doesn't?) But there was much that I needed to learn about prayer as it related to disciple building. At one point one of my sons decided to become the poster child for *The Prodigal Son Campaign*.[6] (I can joke about this now.) At the time, however, it was painful to see him making choices that I knew might jeopardize his life and future. It was also embarrassing and awkward to be the leader of a ministry devoted to disciple building and have one of my primary disciples in a "far-off country." Needless to say there was much consternation and grief.

There were many contributing factors to the situation which I cannot elaborate on here, but suffice it to say that we had raised our son according to Biblical principles and the approaches to disciple building set forth in this and other publications. As I went down my mental Life Coach checklist of these five initiatives, I kept asking the question, "Did I forget or fail to apply something?"

I would be lying if I did not confess that I am an imperfect Life Coach and father. I have made a host of mistakes with all my children. But I sensed there was another factor, beyond my own human frailty, that was contributing to the situation. My son was under spiritual attack by Satan. I soon realized that

when he left home, I was left with only one Life Coaching initiative at my disposal: prayer. I was no longer able to hang out with him, and he had already heard all the truth I could teach. He was no longer interested in me holding him accountable, and I had no leverage for constructing life situations to facilitate his development. So having eliminated all other options, I prayed.

In a matter of days God created specific teaching situations that compelled my son to see truth in a new way. God also set up scenarios that exposed the lies of the enemy and those who espoused them. Many of the Christian convictions that he had held before he left home, reemerged and were stronger. The relationship we had both worked so hard to build and maintain was once again vital. He returned home wiser, and I came to appreciate in a deeper way the importance of prayer as a disciple building initiative.

There was a moment in the training of The Twelve when pride and self-sufficiency had gripped them. They even argued about which of them "was considered to be greatest." Jesus used the occasion to exhort them about true greatness and the link to humility and service. It had gotten to the point where Satan had actually gained some control in Peter's life. We pick up the narrative in the Gospel of Luke where the Lord admonishes, "Simon, Simon, Satan has asked to sift you as wheat. But I have *prayed for you, Simon,* (emphasis mine) that your faith may not fail."

Of course, Peter *was* sifted. He denied that he knew Christ three times as the Lord had predicted and then wept bitterly at his failure. But it is important to remember that the prayer of Jesus was answered. Peter was restored. This ministry of Christ is not reserved only for the apostles. In John 17 we read that He is also praying for us and another Scripture teaches us that our Lord "always lives to make intercession."(NAS) Paul was continually praying for the churches and also for individual believers. We are also urged to pray for one another.

There are times when only fervent prayer will win the day. I don't think it was by accident that, just before Jesus delivered the Great Commission, He prefaced it by saying, "All authority in heaven and

[6] The Story of the Prodigal Son can be found in Luke 15:11-32.

on earth has been given to Me. *Therefore* go and make disciples..." (emphasis mine). We have been given disciple building authority. Pray to the One who commissioned us and watch Him work in the lives of those you coach.

Construct Growth Situations

Some of the events of the Christian life are divinely arranged by the sovereign initiative of God. These events/circumstances are not under the control of the leader/Life Coach. When this occurs, the role of a wise Life Coach is to understand and cooperate with what God has planned and help the disciple respond in faith.

Other types of situations can be planned or constructed by the Life Coach. These constructed situations are designed to create a faith-building experience for the disciple. We will refer to these constructed situations as "structures." Thus, when the disciple builder plans a specific event and challenges the disciple to be a part, a structure for disciple building has been created.

It is important to note that whether a situation is structured or not, it is nonetheless key in the development of the disciple. Both types of situations can create opportunities for growth. This may have been part of what Paul had in mind when he asserted that he had planted and Apollos had watered but it was God who caused the growth.

For example, we can plan an evangelistic foray into our local community in order to create the opportunity for a disciple to learn how to share her faith. At the same time, opportunities to share our faith are before us constantly, whether they are planned or spontaneously created by the Spirit.

An example from Scripture demonstrates how these two types of situations are related. Matthew 14, Mark 6, Luke 9 and John 6 relate how the Lord and His disciples had made plans to retreat (a structure) from the crowds for some much-needed rest. But rather than remain in the villages, the crowds followed them to a remote location. Having compassion and modifying His plans, Jesus went up on the hill-side and sat down to teach the crowd (another structure). Then He challenged His disciples to feed them all (requiring supposedly yet another structure). This situation raised doubts (irritation?), concerns, and struggles. This test of their faith afforded Jesus the opportunity to perform a great miracle and show Himself again to be God. The setting itself was the backdrop for disciple building. The structure (ministering to the crowds) created the faith-building situation.

A closer reading of this text demonstrates the stress and tension that often accompany the structures and situations of ministry. You can sense the frustration in the disciples' reply to Jesus' command to feed the 5000: "That would take eight months of a man's wages! Are we to go and spend that much on bread and give it to them to eat?" (Mark 6:37) Later the same writer candidly points out (Mark 6:52) that the hearts of the disciples "were hardened" and that they "had not gained any insight from the incident (situation) of the loaves."(NAS) The challenges of the Christian life are not always enjoyable, yet they are always instructive if we are trained/discipled to look past the situation to the wisdom and grace that God provides.

After instructing the disciples to go ahead of Him across the lake, Jesus dismissed the crowds and went to pray on the mountain. While He was praying, the disciples encountered a storm at sea that threatened to swamp their small boat. This situation, which Jesus created by telling them to leave without Him and facilitated through His prayers, created another environment that was designed to humble them and create in them a sense of greater dependency on Him while showcasing His divine power and sovereignty. The trial-at-sea caused their faith to grow.

James affirms this same dynamic when he admonishes that we should "consider it pure joy" whenever we face trials of many kinds because the testing of our faith develops perseverance and perseverance ultimately produces maturity (James 1:2-4) . This progressive development of a mature faith is created by the setting (structure/situation) of struggle. James also points out the importance of "doing" (acting on/obeying) truth. Obedience both implies and requires a setting. Whether structured or spontaneous, a setting is important for growth. The wise disciple builder understands the importance of utilizing these situations to build the faith of a disciple.

The writer of Hebrews explains that even the difficult experiences of the Christian life are like the disciplines of a caring father. He reminds his readers that "all discipline for the moment seems not to be joyful but sorrowful; yet, *to those who have been trained by it*, afterwards it yields the peaceful fruit of righteousness." (NAS) Paul reminded the Corinthians that the hardships he suffered happened so that he might learn not to depend on himself, but on Christ Jesus.

Modern spiritual Life Coaches are more than teachers and friends. They have been entrusted with the same authority Christ had for establishing His Kingdom in the hearts of men (Matthew 28:18). In a similar way we should ask God for wisdom in constructing some faith-building experiences and pray that He will sovereignly create others.

As we have already pointed out, we don't arrive at the point of maturity instantly. The Apostle John addressed first century believers as "little children," "young men," and "fathers" signifying stages of development in the Christian life. The writer of Hebrews made the same point when he lamented that he could not teach the solid-food truths he hoped to teach because the readers were still babies needing "milk." Elsewhere all believers are urged to grow up into the full measure of being just like Christ.

The wise Life Coach will strive to balance these two dynamics of progressive growth and practical initiation. He must apply the initiatives that promote growth while accepting the fact that growth takes time. He must pro-actively develop Life Coaching tactics and plans that are wrapped around the five initiatives. At the same time, he must consider the spiritual age or stage of development of the disciple and patiently wait for the Spirit to use his initiatives to cause growth. A careful study of the ministry of Christ reveals that the earthly training of The Twelve progressed in five phases. These phases, outlined in *Disciple Building: A Biblical Framework*, WDA, and elaborated in another section of this manual, provided a growth platform for the ongoing spiritual development of Christ's disciples.

The modern church needs to recapture both the priority and process of disciple building reflected in the ministry of our Lord: a Life Coaching framework that allowed Him to treat each of His disciples as a unique person with individual needs. Understanding this approach requires wisdom, character and strength, the very commodities Paul mentions in Colossians 1:28-29 that are part of the process of presenting every person complete (mature).

> The Life Coach must apply the initiatives that promote growth while accepting the fact that growth takes time.

The Two Categories Of Life Coaches

I like to describe disciple building as: "meeting people where they are, helping them take the next step®." This implies that everybody is somewhere on the journey of being transformed into Christlikeness. A wise Life Coach understands this process and the unique role she needs to play in helping people grow. To achieve this she needs to be able to address varying needs. We've discovered that there are two different categories of Life Coaches that can be used in a local church to facilitate and encourage spiritual growth: the encouraging coach and the equipping coach.

Needing different coaches to achieve different objectives is not unique to the church. Sports teams often employ different types of coaches who help train and discipline the players. Football teams use line coaches, coaches for defensive and offensive backs, and strength and conditioning coaches. A baseball team deploys hitting coaches, pitching coaches, and coaches to help players who are running the bases. In the church, each type of Life Coach has a unique role and purpose to help believers develop and grow.

The Encouraging Coach

At times, all Christians experience trouble, disappointment, discouragement, or confusion. During these seasons it helps tremendously to have a Christian friend who, either figuratively or literally, puts his arm around our shoulder to offer support, provide perspective, and give encouragement. This coming alongside is a vital part of life in the church. When Jesus spoke of the Holy Spirit, He used the Greek term "paracletos" that's translated, "the one

who comes alongside." The Scriptures promise that God is there for us, "a very present help in trouble." (NAS) And His comfort is more than just the internal indwelling of His Spirit; it is also external through the nearness and encouragement of His people.

An encouraging coach has a ministry of simply "being there" when people need encouragement. A willingness to pray with people going through a difficult time or to listen as they share their struggles is powerful and life changing. Extensive training isn't required for this type of coaching, only a willingness to be available and a compassion to care. The five initiatives mentioned above are a simple mental checklist for how to meet people at their point of need.

Sometimes an encourager is able to do more than minister by being available; there are times when she's able to leverage her own life experience in a strategic way. We've all heard the phrase: "Been there, done that." This usually signifies that someone has actually "been through" whatever the particular topic of discussion might be. Those who have experienced the matter under review usually feel qualified to present their opinion with an air of certainty that can only be derived from having actually "been there" in real life.

For example, someone who's been to a particular amusement park might know where the best parking is located to avoid traffic congestion at closing time. In this case the experience provides valuable information to help a first-time visitor avoid delays. Most of us have both received and given this type of encouraging help. It's probably what the writer of Hebrews meant when he admonished Christians to "spur one another on toward love and good deeds. Let us not give up meeting together, as some are in the habit of doing, but let us encourage one another—and all the more as you see the Day approaching." (Hebrews 10:24-25) It's what Paul meant when he urged us to bear one another's burdens.

In a church, encouraging coaches might have experience at raising children, working with teens, staying out of debt, working from a budget, surviving a business failure, or dealing with chronic illness. Sometimes the experience most needed is grief support or marriage tips or small group dynamics. The list of needs can be as vast and varied as our life experiences, but in each case the key ingredient is that the encouraging coach is able to come alongside and help at a particular point of need.

People who can most use the help of someone who's "been there, done that" are looking for Life Coaching tips to help them through a similar life situation. The primary qualifications for this type of Life Coach are: personal experience, commitment, and enough concern and availability to "come alongside and encourage" the person they're trying to help. Encouragers help others seek Christ as they put into practice the wisdom of what worked for them.

Church leaders are able to assign and deploy these encouraging coaches to help other believers in specific areas. Yet there are some kinds of needs that require extra training and experience. This leads to a discussion of the other type of Life Coach: the equipping coach.

The Equipping Coach

When my children were small, a big Saturday at the Dukes' house featured breakfast at a national chain restaurant. In addition to the fast-food cuisine, the visit also included a trip to the playground with its corkscrew plastic tubes and pits filled with multi-colored rubber balls. After the last crumb was washed down with orange juice, I would announce,

> An encouraging coach has a ministry of simply "being there" when people need encouragement.

"You've got twenty-five seconds." This was the signal to launch our game of "Monster-in-the-Maze," a wild romp where they would hide and I would try to catch them. Bolting out of the booth they would dive into the play area and I would follow, growling and tickling. This lasted until we had to run errands, or I got winded—usually the latter.

One Saturday after the antics Jesse, my youngest son, asked, "Dad, are there any *real* monsters?" I sensed this was not a hypothetical issue having recently discovered Jesse in bed with me after bouts with bad dreams. Rather than quickly respond, I tossed the issue back to him, "What do you think?" He replied, "Well, Dad, probably not the kind we can see." What followed was a discussion of Satan and spiritual warfare. It was natural to also mention faith in Christ, our Strong Deliverer and Captain of the Armies of Heaven. Older sister Elissa then queried, "Dad, is this stuff *really* true, or just another one of your stories?" Here was another opportunity for world-view and faith formation, a complex process that addresses the great questions of life. This training happens best in everyday situations.

As the children grew, we moved on to other activities, but the format was the same: we would do something together and then talk about what was going on in our lives. Soccer games, canoe trips, piano recitals, and mountain retreats were combined with time to reflect. Truth was unpacked as the experiences of our lives formed the context for discussion. But as they matured, the content deepened. Some of the activities with my daughters were different than the boys, but the format was the same. We lived life together. As we raised children, Linda and I would 'coach' them along the way. At times the relational stakes were pretty high. During those tricky teen years, we had to use some tough love by setting boundaries and holding the lines.

What is true for parents is true for spiritual Life Coaches. Experienced disciple builders understand that new believers need a spiritual diet that is different from those who have walked with the Lord for many years. New Testament writers capture this concept when they refer to the need for "milk" for babies and "meat" for the more mature. Other places in Scripture make reference to broad developmental growth patterns.

Sometimes people experience growth spurts when God reveals new truths and the relationship with Him rockets forward. These periods are often followed by seasons of dormancy. During the winter months a tree may appear dead to the casual observer, but it is actually absorbing the nutrients acquired during the growing season and expanding its root system. In the same way our spiritual growth goes through periods of expansion and assimilation. No two of us grow at exactly the same rate, yet we all grow in similar stages. Life Coaches therefore need to adopt a progressive posture when they relate to those they will lead. The first step in the process is understanding that maturity does develop over time, and we must adapt our approach to accommodate the spiritual age of the disciple. We also need to remember what was mentioned earlier: the need to balance method and mystery. We plant and water, but the Holy Spirit causes growth.

As a disciple develops and changes, the role of the Life Coach needs to change in the same way that the role of a parent changes. At each point in the process the disciple building goals must be adjusted. Relationships move from being casual and formative at the beginning to a point where the bond between the disciple-builder and disciple is incredibly close. Eventually, the wise Life Coach will understand that the relationship usually moves from disciple-builder to disciple and then to one of being peers. This is apparently what happened in the relationship between Barnabas and Paul. Barnabas accepted Paul and loved him, tutoring him in the faith until the time came when they needed to part ways to form independent ministries. Eventually Paul passed the 'discipleship baton' on to Timothy.

How The Roles Of An Equipping Coach Change

The Phases and Types of Equipping Relationships

A careful study of *A Harmony of the Gospels*[7] reveals that our Lord was following a pattern in developing His ministry and training His disciples. There are distinct pivot points when Jesus issued new challenges to His band of disciples, or embarked on new initiatives of outreach. Each of these pivot points signals a change in His disciple building approach and marks a new phase in the development of those who followed Him. Not all of His disciples progressed at the same pace, but there was movement toward maturity. Other New Testament writers also emphasize the dynamic of progressive spiritual development.

There are five distinct phases of formative spiritual development that are based on the ministry training model of Christ. Each phase has its own goals and objectives. God has specific things He wants to accomplish in each of our lives, but the broad goals are the same for everyone. In the same way that children must crawl before they walk, disciples must progress developmentally to be spiritually healthy. It is important that we understand the order. The role of a Life Coach also needs to change as the spiritual maturation process progresses.[8]

Christ's relationships with The Twelve serve as models in helping us know generally how our relationships with our disciples need to change as they grow. As time passes and the disciple grows in Christlikeness, the personal relationship between the Life Coach and the disciple progresses from a more casual, formative relationship to a deeper team-building partnership until eventually they become ministry peers with the disciple moving on to establish an independent ministry.

At Phase I the relationship is casual and informal as relationships are built and trust is established. It is important to let the disciple know your reason for a specific appointment (e.g. to talk about the claims of Christ, etc.), but there is no established, ongoing commitment for the disciple or Life Coach.

At Phase II the relationship continues to develop as the disciple and Life Coach meet occasionally or in the context of a small group. Appointments can be arranged to just check in or perhaps to meet a felt need. One of the roles of the Life Coach is to help the disciple find a friend/partner who is at or near the same level of maturity. As growth continues, more formal appointments built around intentional growth projects can be arranged.

At Phase III a disciple is in Equipping for Ministry and the commitment level (to the group and to the Life Coach) has increased. At this point, a regular

---

[7] See *A Harmony of the Gospels*, A.T. Robertson or *A Harmony of the Four Gospels: The New International Version*, Orville E. Daniel.

[8] For more information on the progressive ministry of Christ, see *Disciple Building: A Biblical Framework*, WDA.

appointment can be set up (once per week or once every two weeks). Of course, informal, unscheduled times together do much to build the relationship. In addition, there is team training time.

In Phase IV the focus and specificity of the time spent together increases as the relationship develops. However, in Phase V, although the responsibility and therefore the commitment increases, the amount of time spent together decreases. This is the time when the disciple is being weaned from dependence on the Life Coach and given more independence. The disciple is rising to work alongside the Life Coach during this phase and becomes more of a partner in ministry.

Phase I: The Evangelistic Life Coach

The first phase of development is the new birth experience, the point at which a disciple comes to believe in Jesus as the Christ, the Lord from Heaven. Faith is established, and there is redemption from spiritual darkness and bondage into a true understanding of God and His Kingdom. Paul describes this transition in the first chapter of Colossians where he states that we have been qualified to share in the Kingdom of light, He rescued us "from the dominion of darkness and brought us into the Kingdom of the Son." In another place, he says this transition is more than simply being enlightened mentally. It actually involves a new birth, when we move from being "dead in [our] transgressions and sins" and by nature "objects of wrath" to being alive in Him. "But because of His great love for us, God, who is rich in mercy, made us alive with Christ even when we were dead." (Ephesians 2:1,4) This is what Jesus was explaining to Nicodemus in John 3.

This process of being made alive is a great mystery accomplished by the regenerating work of God's Holy Spirit. We are told in Romans 10 that God appoints messengers to deliver His message of truth. The first type of Life Coach, therefore, is the evangelist. In the letter to the Ephesians, Paul asserts that in the church God has appointed evangelists, people who have a gift for being able to communicate the good news about Christ to those who need to hear.

Most of us, when we think of an evangelist, think of Billy Graham. Certainly Dr. Graham has been used mightily by God in much the same way that God used John the Baptist. These types of evangelists are able to communicate truth to large audiences.

But for every Billy Graham there are hundreds of people like Everette Albrecht, someone who does not fit the mold of a typical evangelist. Quiet and unassuming, you might be tempted to discount the impact he has made on the lives of hundreds of college students. For many in the Purdue University community, he was the person who first helped them come to faith in Christ. They know him from chatting over a cup of coffee at a fraternity house or from walking in the woods while hunting deer or from attending a small group Bible study on campus. Everette is an evangelistic Life Coach.

The Evangelistic Life Coach is the person who is able to establish a relationship with an unbeliever and present the claims of Christ in a direct but sensitive way. The goal for the Evangelistic Life Coach is not just to present the message, but establish a credible witness. This witness includes a real life relationship that communicates concern and commitment. Often these relationships can last for years before the person finally accepts Christ.

For the Evangelistic Life Coach to be successful she must go to unbelievers, not wait for unbelievers to come to her. This will involve stepping outside the comfortable or familiar environment of the local church and going into the world, establishing relational connections with people who don't know the Lord. Jesus was accused of being a "friend of sinners" because he established relationships with unbelievers. We must do the same. This doesn't mean we should embrace sinful lifestyles, but it does mean we must befriend people who don't follow Christ. This can occur by socializing with health club members after a workout, joining a secular book club, or volunteering with the PTO.

For more adventurous types, it might involve something more risky. Our modern evangelical subculture has stigmatized certain kinds of people as social outcasts in the same way the Pharisees labeled and avoided the outcasts of their day. Jesus, without condoning their sins, was able to establish trust relationships with tax-collectors, Samaritan women, lepers, and prostitutes. Not everyone Jesus related to in this way came to believe in Him, but many did. Some modern Evangelistic Life Coaches will find a way to connect with those who are socially and spiritually dis-enfranchised and lead many of them to Christ.

Phase II: The Foundations Life Coach

Once a person has accepted Christ, he needs help getting established in his new life of faith. Sometimes the person who leads someone to Christ is also the person who can help the new believer get started in the Christian life. (If the relationship already exists, it is natural to capitalize and build on this.) But a Life Coach with the gift of evangelism is often more concerned about leading people to Christ than he is about helping the new believer get grounded. A different kind of Life Coaching relationship is required and this might involve a relationship with a new Life Coach.

The new believer needs to be nurtured and trained. Now the goal is to establish a solid foundation for the new faith. This requires helping him turn away from old lifestyles to embrace new values and new choices. There is a legitimate need for the new believer to bond with his new spiritual family, establish a relational network and create a sense of emotional connectedness. He is learning to identify needs, deal with his emotions, and turn away from unhealthy addictions and habits.

This phase also involves teaching the basic truths of the Christian life and offering a new perspective on the world. Spiritual disciplines, such as devotions and prayer, need to be introduced. They should be presented as a means to pursuing a fresh relationship with a God who is personal and intimate. Questions will need answers, doubts will need to be addressed, and stumblings will require both admonition and patience. The Life Coach will have to pursue and take

> For the Evangelistic Life Coach to be successful she must go to unbelievers, not wait for unbelievers to come to her.

the initiative without crowding or becoming pushy or demanding.

This is the best time to begin a small group in which several Christians who are just beginning the Christian life can grow together. The Life Coach who is also a small group leader has several advantages. He is able to utilize group dynamics and camaraderie to facilitate growth and help introduce the young believer into community, an important element of life in the Body of Christ. In addition, the small group members are able to learn about and discuss Scripture, another vital ingredient for nurture.

But small group time alone will not suffice. The young believer needs individual attention from someone who is able to provide encouragement and perspective during this early time in the disciple building process. He is vulnerable to spiritual attacks and easy prey for the one Peter says "prowls around like a roaring lion looking for someone to devour." (I Peter 5:8) The Foundations Life Coach is critical in helping to protect and establish the young believer in the same way a shepherd guards the young lambs.

The modern evangelical community has often been shortsighted when it comes to helping new believers get established. By pushing them into ministry responsibilities too soon, before their foundational concrete has hardened, we put them at risk. Without solid foundations they can be unprepared for the challenges they will face later in the Christian life. This is not to say that new believers cannot be strategically involved in the ministry. But the Life Coach should exercise caution before allowing the disciple to assume more responsibility than he is ready to handle.

Young believers can be strategically involved in the ministry without being over-challenged. Most young believers still have many good friends who are not yet Christians. This is a golden moment in many of these relationships where the new believer still retains influence and trust. A wise Life Coach will capitalize on these relationships and attempt to help the new believer's friends also establish faith in Christ while helping the new disciple understand that his primary responsibility is to grow. God has set forth in Scripture a balanced way for this to occur.

A significant step of faith and development occurs when the new believer is able to publicly declare his intention to follow Christ. The Scripture uses the term baptism to describe the new relationship we have with Christ and His church. In the same way we are saturated with water, we have become cleansed by and immersed in Christ. For some traditions the experience of baptism involves having the believer participate in a special service where the focus is on the declaration of commitment to Christ. Not all evangelical traditions treat baptism the same way, but most admit there is a need for the new believer to proclaim his new faith publicly.

Most modern baptisms occur in the relative privacy of a church sanctuary, though some occur outdoors. For first century Christians, baptism took place where there was water available in the community, usually in public places of high visibility. This public declaration often resulted in others embracing Christ and validating the new believer's faith. At other times this public proclamation caused people to reject the new believer. Today old friends may accept Christ or become increasingly uncomfortable in their relationship with the new believer. This period results in the new believer finding a new set of friends—fellow Christians in the church.

As he becomes more involved in the life of the community, a subtle but very powerful dynamic begins to occur. The disciple begins to understand that he is part of a greater Kingdom and purpose. This revelation provides substantial emotional support as he understands that he is no longer the "old man" of his past. He has become "a new man" in Christ with new values and a new purpose.

> As he becomes more involved in the life of the community, a subtle but very powerful dynamic begins to occur. The disciple begins to understand that he is part of a greater Kingdom and purpose.

The challenge for the Life Coach is to encourage an appropriate level of ministry involvement and commitment balanced by the need to grow and develop. A wise father will allow his young son to visit his workplace and perhaps participate in some limited activities. This experience builds confidence, vision and motivation. But he will not allow him to assume responsibilities in the work place beyond his level of maturity.

This is also the time when new habits and disciplines need to be established as part of the new foundation for growth. The Life Coach can emphasize the importance of a daily quiet time and help the young believer find appropriate devotional guides and materials. WDA has a set of materials to assist the Life Coach as he helps the young believer develop a root system for further growth. (More information and a curriculum for the *Laying Foundations Experience* are available from WDA.)

Phase III: The Equipping for Ministry Life Coach

There does come a time when a disciple needs to be equipped for and involved actively in ministry. This equipping includes teaching her how to share her testimony and the gospel. Jesus said, "Follow me, and I will make you become fishers of men." Jesus was constantly engaged in spiritual warfare which served as the backdrop for much of His teaching about worldview development and about the conflict between the kingdom of light and darkness. The enemy will not remain idle as we move to set the captives free, spoiling his efforts to keep people in bondage. But the attacks of the evil one are used by God to reveal more about His sovereignty and power over evil in all its forms.

When young believers reach this equipping stage of spiritual development, it is appropriate to expand the base of the ministry by striving to reach another generation of disciples. The reaching of a new generation accomplishes two strategic objectives. Besides achieving the goal of 1) proclaiming Christ and making new disciples, it also serves to 2) strengthen the faith of those being trained in ministry, providing practical experiences in reaching others.

The training in evangelism (and all subsequent training) is best accomplished if the Life Coach utilizes a **four-stage process of transfer** that is summarized with the acronym **OPSI**: **O**bservation, **P**articipation, **S**upervision, and **I**ndependence. In the first stage the disciple accompanies the Life Coach and merely *observes* while the Life Coach shares the gospel. In the second stage, the disciple *participates* in some meaningful way such as sharing a brief personal testimony. In the third stage the disciple initiates the action while the Life Coach *supervises* the event, offering critical input later. In the final stage the disciple initiates *independently* of the Life Coach and reports back after the action.

This pattern of transfer is reflected in what Jesus did. He initially challenged His disciples to accompany Him on the mission to upper Galilee and eventually commissioned them to conduct evangelistic forays into new communities independent of Him.

The way the stages of transfer are used will depend on the disciple and the circumstances. Some disciples will need more observation time and feedback; others will need less. Be creative and flexible, keeping the goals in mind. For example, it may be difficult to arrange a situation in which the disciple can observe you as a Life Coach. A less ideal alternative is for you to go over the planning of the situation with the disciple and then communicate in detail the specifics, including your thoughts during the situation and how and why you did what you did.

Team Ministry: The benefits of utilizing all the gifts of the church

Jesus challenged more than one of the disciples in His group to become "fishers of men." This group training experience was more efficient and afforded a team dynamic. It is ideal if the Life Coach also utilizes this team approach, though this is not always possible. If no team experience is available the disci-

ple builder should take advantage of ministry opportunities that exist within the larger ministry of the local church or community. By utilizing standing ministries such as outreach teams and homeless shelters, or taking advantage of periodic evangelistic events such as community-wide outreaches, the Life Coach is able to provide evangelistic experiences without having to create a team dynamic.

The Life Coach does not have to be gifted or effective at evangelism for this phase to be successful. The disciple can be assigned to work alongside someone who has the gift of evangelism in order to learn the skills and share the experience. But remember that besides being called to build disciples, we are also charged to continue growing ourselves. God rewards our faithfulness even if we do not have the gift mix that is best suited for the training objective. Paul urged Timothy to do the work of an evangelist whether he had the gift or not.

In addition to addressing the proclamation of the Gospel, this Equipping for Ministry Experience should also include instruction in the critical principles of Christian life appropriate for this stage of maturity. Some of these include: our new identity in Christ, the new freedom we have as believers, and issues such as "law versus grace" and the need for healthy relationships. It is also interesting to note that Christ often dealt with many unaddressed emotional needs in the life of His disciples by incorporating them into His new spiritual family. Their involvement with Him, in the adventure of extending the Kingdom of His Father, caused them to develop a more healthy sense of their significance and importance.

Phase IV: The New Leader Life Coach

There was a time in the ministry of Jesus when He sent out The Twelve independently. This event was a pivot point in His ministry as He began to utilize The Twelve as definitive leaders in His ministry movement. In a similar way this is the time in the life of a contemporary disciple when he needs to assume leadership responsibilities both in the overall movement and in the lives of individual disciples.

This training is different from being trained in ministry skills. In this stage the disciple accepts ongoing responsibility for the spiritual development of others. Similarly the Life Coach now assumes more responsibility. In addition to helping his disciple grow and develop, the Life Coach also indirectly takes on responsibility for helping his disciple help a new disciple (who has just entered the Foundations Phase) begin to grow. If the disciple (now a New Leader) experienced a healthy Foundations Experience himself, he will be in a good position to help someone else lay solid foundations.

At this point in the process we begin to see disciple building multiplication take place. In II Timothy chapters 1-2, Paul admonishes young Timothy to keep "the pattern of sound teaching" that Paul had received from Christ. Just a few verses later he goes on to spell out the very things Timothy had learned from Paul that he should "entrust these to faithful men who would be able to teach others also."(NAS) The Life Coach can begin to explain to the new leader that there is indeed a progressive pattern of teaching or disciple building that he has been following to equip the disciple. In the next section we will discuss a flexible disciple building framework (the *R-CAPS* approach) that has been proven beneficial as a ministry development planning tool and training guide.

At this phase we reemphasize the value of learning truth by being placed in situations of responsibility. (This is where those being coached become coaches themselves.) Serving as a newly appointed Life Coach, especially if this assignment occurs in a team of other new leaders, provides the context for new truths to be learned and for new faith steps to be taken.

Much of the teaching about body life and the priority of eternal matters over temporal matters occurs at this stage, forged in the fire of difficult ministry challenges. Some of these challenges happen naturally as people work closely together. Other challenges seem to be sovereignly designed by Jesus for the purpose of testing strongly held (but false) assumptions about ministry and Kingdom life.

This period of reevaluation causes disciples to rework their expectations regarding the Christian life.

They are forced to sort out what is good and bad about life, a complex but very important part of the process of becoming mature believers. Also addressed is the tension of balancing the concept that the Kingdom is both "now" and "not yet," an issue that has prompted heated denominational debate. The Life Coach plays a critical role in this environment, and relational trust becomes paramount.

This is the point in the ministry of Christ when, according to Scripture, "many of His disciples turned back and no longer followed Him." (John 6:66) We're not told exactly what this meant, but it certainly involved a point of serious reevaluation of ministry priorities and values. This is also the time when the disciples who remained gained new and deeper insight into God's mission and purpose.

Phase V: The Mature Leader Life Coach

I hope it has become evident by now that you are teaching your disciples to do everything you have already done with them. Your example coupled with their experiences should have provided a solid foundation for them to repeat the process. But there are additional truths and experiences that cannot be fully appropriated until they also go through the process of leading others.

At this stage in the disciple building process the Life Coach helps the disciple, who has developed into a Life Coach herself, become even more effective by learning to lead other leaders. This is the stage in the ministry of Christ when He appointed The Seventy as a new generation of leaders. They now joined The Twelve in the leadership training process. The original band of disciples began to assume more leadership responsibilities for the overall ministry administration, including helping to supervise and direct the activities of the newly-appointed The Seventy. This situation created opportunities for growth, but it also was the flash point for conflict and potential disunity.

As leadership responsibility grows, pride often grows with it. In Jesus' ministry this resulted in arguments over "who was the greatest." The modern

Life Coach needs to be prepared for ministry "turf wars" and relational conflicts among the leadership team. Jesus capitalized on the relational pressure to give perspective regarding the priority and power of agape love that produces unity. He also stressed the importance of servant leadership, reviewed His role as the suffering (but conquering) Messiah who would be raised to a position of all-authority, and promised the enabling power of the Holy Spirit when human effort falls short. All these truths had undoubtedly been discussed before, but the advanced leader development situation served as the catalyst for new teaching opportunities. He also used the occasion to teach them how to handle persecution, as opposition to Him became highly focused.

Some Christian counselors remind us that a key transition point for adolescents moving into adult life involves "weaning" them from adult supervision. Perhaps the most important faith step at this phase of disciple building occurs as the leaders/disciples are given more responsibility and more freedom by the Life Coach. This prepares them for the transition to full independence. The Life Coach must model servant leadership and not hold too tightly to her own ministry role, since this is the point when the leaders/disciples become mature ministry peers primed for deployment. They either leave to form new works or assume key roles that may have been originally held by the Life Coach.

Dynamics of a "Team of Life Coaches"

There is great value when one Life Coach working alone is able to help someone else grow. But there is a tremendous advantage when a team of Life Coaches can work together to help several disciples develop. Of course, this team dynamic is not always

> There is a tremendous advantage when a team of Life Coaches can work together to help several disciples develop.

possible because of logistical constraints, but we should endeavor to create such an environment whenever practical. This is apparently what Paul had in mind in Ephesians chapter 4 when he outlined the various leadership roles and functions of church leadership. Though their gifts are different, all of the leaders mentioned in this passage share the responsibility of building the church and equipping the disciples. The outcome was a disciple building process that produced the twin-fruits of effective ministry (i.e. works of service) and growth of the body toward Christlike maturity.

Whenever there is a team dynamic several beneficial things take place. First, there is the advantage of having several people focused together on the task of building disciples. Scripture teaches that where there is an "abundance of counselors," (NAS) war is waged wisely, and victory is assured. We have already spoken of the realities of spiritual warfare associated with the disciple building process. In Ecclesiastes the writer extols the merits of two or more laboring together, especially citing the ability to resist an opponent. This multi-perspective approach also helps balance extremes of personality, experience, and giftedness. In addition, the specific needs of a disciple are easier to discern when there is a team in place to give feedback.

Most people I know are incredibly busy and stressed from work and family responsibilities. The thought of adding another church responsibility to an already saturated schedule seems overwhelming. One of the biggest hurdles of the Life Coach process is finding the time to invest in someone else. Another advantage of the team approach is the benefit of a shared labor pool. This works especially well if two Life Coaches can team up to lead a small group. In a group of eight this means that each of the leaders is responsible for four disciples.[9]

Spiritual giftedness does play a role in the Life Coach process. We mentioned earlier that someone with the gift of evangelism may not be the best Life Coach for the Foundations Experience. Conversely,

---

[9] See *Small Groups Manual* (WDA) for more information regarding shared leadership of a small group.

someone with the gift of Pastor-Teacher may not be as enthusiastic about evangelism as someone with that gift. (This may have been what prompted Paul to admonish young pastor Timothy to fulfill his ministry responsibilities by doing "the work of an evangelist.") Sometimes we don't have the luxury of operating exclusively in the area of our giftedness. But when this is possible we should take advantage of the situation.

How this works out practically is that we are able to "loan" our disciples to someone else on the leadership team who can equip them in areas in which we may be less proficient. But for this to be most effective, the original Life Coach needs to retain the responsibility for the growth and development of the disciple. (In WDA we refer to this as "holding the project book" on the disciple.) This helps to prevent a disciple from "getting lost in the shuffle" that sometimes occurs in a busy ministry. This process of transferring training roles and developing projects will become clearer when we discuss how to design individual disciple building projects for those we Life Coach.

Another benefit to the team approach in Life Coaching is that the disciples are able to see a team dynamic modeled. Most of us learn best in an environment in which we can both hear and see truth being applied. This dynamic becomes very important at Phase IV: Developing New Leaders and Phase V: Developing Mature Leaders. There are relational tensions that inevitably develop as the stresses of ministry encroach. Watching the Life Coach team handle these challenges is vital for the faith development of the emerging leaders. For this reason each individual team Life Coach should be braced for and expectant of the spiritual warfare that will be part of the team experience.

Changing Life Coaches

There may come a time when it becomes necessary to change the Life Coach relationship completely. This can be caused by a variety of factors. Sometimes the schedules or lifestyles of either disciple or Life Coach change so that it becomes impractical for the process to continue. Sometimes the seasons of life dictate change. We have already mentioned the giftedness factor that can be addressed somewhat by a team approach. But sometimes, especially if a team is not available, it becomes helpful if the disciple can find a Life Coach who has a gift-mix that is more similar to his own. It may become evident that there are needs in the life of a disciple that cannot be adequately addressed by the Life Coach. This may be due to a lack of experience or training. There may have been emotional or relational damage from the past that necessitates special counseling. In this case, the Life Coach may be unable to provide the best support system.

Life Coaching: A Practical Strategy

Using the *NGP (Needs-Goals-Projects) Approach*

Now that we have explored the Life Coach role, we will turn our attention to a tool that can be used by a Life Coach to encourage someone to grow. This tool is called an NGP, an acronym for Needs-Goals-Projects, which helps a Life Coach know how to discern Needs, set Goals and write Projects. It is useful in training leaders to pray through, think through, write, and then implement a personalized disciple building strategy. Having a strategy in building disciples will help prevent aimlessness and communication overload.

Before we begin with the *NGP* tool, you need to be introduced to the *Christian Growth Checklist (CGC)* on page 67. This *Checklist,* which is used along with the *NGP* tool, was designed to assist a Life Coach and a disciple discover specific spiritual growth needs. The *Checklist* helps measure maturity and identify needs along a progressive growth continuum. This growth continuum is linked to the training grid *(R-CAPS Grid)* developed from researching the disciple building methods of Christ. The Grid tracks spiritual development through five phases of formative disciple building growth, from initial faith formations through advanced leadership training. The *CGC* is designed to identify personal needs in various sectors of life including (but not limited to) theological understanding, ministry skills, leadership, emotional development, worldview, relational abilities, and faith development.

Step 1: Discover the Needs of a Disciple

The well-known psychologist A. H. Maslow sug-gested that there is a hierarchy of human needs. We need to be fed and clothed; we need to feel secure; we need companionship and love; we need to understand our purpose and the meaning of life; and we need to feel that we are a significant part of the world. Each of these areas can be expanded further. (E.g., in order to feel good physically, we need to take care of our bodies.) Accordingly, some of our needs are felt (i.e., we are aware of them and desire to meet them), while others are unfelt (i.e., we are unaware of the need). In Exhibit D you will find a *Needs Worksheet* which provides a list of needs by category to be considered when writing an *NGP.*

For example, parents experience this tension between felt and unfelt needs all the time. Little Susie wants to stay up past her bedtime. She has a felt need to have fun and be entertained by her favorite pastimes. Mom, realizing Susie also has an unfelt need for rest (even though Susie insists that she is not tired), lies down beside her and reads a book to her. Within minutes, Susie's unfelt need has become her felt need. She is sound asleep.

To be effective as disciple builders (Life Coaches), we must be skilled at discerning and interpreting needs. Part of discovering needs involves soliciting the disciple's assistance. A good Life Coach will assess the disciple's situation accurately by listening carefully and asking questions. Some felt needs can lead us to discover underlying unfelt needs. Once again we must stress that a trust relationship is imperative for good results. If a disciple is convinced that the leader has her interests in mind and is concerned for her welfare, she will be more eager to share needs and to work toward allowing

Christ to address these needs so she will grow toward maturity.

Emotional and spiritual needs are often the most difficult to define. Because our society embraces a materialistic worldview, the worth of the individual within our culture is determined primarily by a temporal system of values (i.e., what he can do or achieve). Feelings of estrangement and erosion of self-worth are becoming a by-product of our age. Only a reprogramming of our mental perception of self, aligned along a Biblical perspective, will produce emotionally healthy people.

Because God has given us a pattern for ministry (Christ's training of The Twelve), we can discern needs based on where a person is in the developmental pattern. For example, a person who is at "Phase II: Laying Foundations" (see *R-CAPS Grid*) has a need to develop a personal relationship with God – to learn to trust Him and communicate with Him. Conversely, if we notice that a person is struggling in his personal relationship with God, it is probable that, even though he may have been a Christian for years, he is still dealing with issues characteristic of a young believer.

The *R-CAPS Grid* encapsulates the process of disciple building. This model should prove helpful in understanding where a disciple is (what she needs) in her spiritual development and in identifying broad goals for each level of spiritual development. The *Christian Growth Checklist (CGC)* described above is helpful in identifying many of the specific needs associated with each stage of growth and suggests certain approaches helpful in meeting these needs (projects).

After you familiarize yourself with the variety of needs (using the *CGC*, *R-CAPS Grid* and *Needs Worksheet*), you are ready to begin to discern and record the needs of your disciple. As you read through the categories, ask yourself questions such as, "Is this a need in my disciple's life?" If so, "How strong is the need?" The following guidelines will be helpful:

1. Approach the task of discerning needs with prayer for wisdom.

2. Remember: LOVE is primary (I Corinthians 14:1 and I Peter 4:8).

3. Your discernment will become clearer as you know your disciple better. Therefore, spend time with your disciple in various situations.

4. To avoid negativism and affirm the positive, think in terms of your disciple's strengths as well as needs.

5. Remember to respect your disciple's privacy and reputation. Share your thoughts only with a person who needs to know in order to help.

6. Remember: Although this may be difficult at first, experience helps. Commit it to the Lord, be diligent to do your best and trust Him with the results.

Later, when thinking about needs has become natural and automatic for you, going through each category step-by-step will not be necessary.

We will focus on a man named "Mark" as we walk through the process of writing an *NGP*. Mark is a fictional young man, but his characteristics and challenges are typical of many young men in our churches. To help you better understand the process of designing growth projects, we want to give you a realistic example. Let us introduce you to Mark.

Meet Mark.

Mark is a thirty-five-year-old man who works as a project manager for a computer company. He is married and has two children: six years and three years old.

As a teenager Mark made a commitment to Christ, but was not serious about his relationship with God until a year ago. Since then he has been in a small group Bible study on the book of John and has grown steadily: learning to spend time with the Lord, learning to walk obediently with Christ, and seeing Christ meet his needs. This past year he has worked with the group of men that have the responsibility of keeping up the church building and landscaping.

Recently Mark has begun to be concerned for several of his fellow workers who are not believers and are missing out on a personal relationship with Jesus. He has expressed this concern to some of his Christian friends, but he has also mentioned his sense of inadequacy in sharing with non-Christians.

Mark and his wife, Marsha, have a good relationship. However, at times the many demands of having young children hinder them from maintaining good communication. Also, Mark works long hours. He says that he is committed to spending time with his family, but often allows his work to rob time from them. He and Marsha have had some arguments about his long working hours and neglecting his family.

Mark relates easily to people and has a servant heart. He is known as a loyal friend and at times has trouble saying "no" when his friends ask him to do things for them.

First, Discover Mark's Needs.

We all have felt and unfelt needs, equipping needs, emotional and relational needs (restorative), physical needs, etc. To help discern Mark's needs, we talk with him (to come up with the Case Study), look over the *Needs Worksheet*, and have him complete the *Christian Growth Checklist (CGC)*. (You will find the *CGC* in the Exhibit on page 67 and the *Needs Worksheet* on page 81.) All three of these means help us get to know Mark better, but regardless of the method of determining needs, God the Holy Spirit is the Revealer of needs.

In Exhibit F you will find the results of Mark's *CGC*. Looking at the two pages from the Equipping portion, notice that he checked every item in Phase II which indicates that the Foundation phase of his faith has been laid and is solid. The Equipping for Ministry Phase, on the other hand, has only a few checked items. This tells us that Mark's equipping needs are at Phase III. He is ready and needs to be equipped

to begin to have a ministry. Some (not all) of the needs he has are:

- The need to learn to share his faith (*CGC* items #32, 36, 43)

- The need to learn how to lead an evangelistic Bible study (#33)

- The need to learn to share his testimony (#35)

- The need to learn how to help a new believer begin to grow (#44)

- The need to have a more consistent devotional time (#40)

- The need to learn to study the Scripture in a systematic way (#39)

There are also two pages from the Restorative portion of the *CGC*. Notice that many of the items in Phase II are not checked. So we can conclude that although Mark is at Phase III in the equipping areas, he actually has needs at an earlier phase (Phase II) in the restorative areas of his life.

The discrepancy between equipping development and restorative development is not surprising. Mark is quite typical of many believers. Too often restorative issues (emotional and relational health) lag behind the development of equipping skills. Even though restorative issues are vital to personal growth, they often receive little attention in our culture and especially in our churches. In fact, the topic may be totally new to some individuals. Unfortunately, when restorative issues are not addressed they can hinder all growth.

Looking at Mark's Case Study and *CGC* (restorative portion) we note that he may have a work addiction that causes problems for him and his family. It is not uncommon for people to use addictions to medicate, numb or distract themselves from their emotions. We also see that Mark has difficulty saying "no" to people which results in others taking advantage of him. This may indicate that he has an underlying restorative issue such as having an inordinate need for approval. We also can see that Mark may not deal with his emotions in a healthy way.

It may be possible for Mark to solve these problems by simply making better decisions. However, it is much more likely that he will need to deal directly with the restorative issues in his life that have not been addressed and are causing these difficulties. (For more information about restorative issues, see *How Emotional Problems Develop*, available from WDA.[10]) These insights lead us to Mark's needs, which include

- The need to "get in touch" with his emotions (to understand and learn to express them) (*CGC* items #11, 12, 18, 19, 20, 22)

- The need to learn to set boundaries with other people (say "no") (#33, 36, 50, 53, 54)

- The need to face and deal with his addiction to work (#16)

Step 2: Prioritize the Needs of a Disciple

The list of needs you have identified may be quite lengthy. Obviously, not all needs can be focused on at once. At this point, prioritizing becomes important. How do you decide which needs need to be addressed first? Your choice should be influenced by:

1. Your understanding of where the disciple is in his spiritual development. (For example, is evangelism the most important need, or does he need to establish a broader theological base first? Maybe his fear will dissipate as he understands the greatness of Christ.)

2. A ministry in the church that the disciple can benefit from participating in. (Is there an

evangelism outreach planned where he can be encouraged to give his testimony, etc.?)

3. Your personal circumstances and the circumstances of the disciple. (Are you able to create a natural situation for modeling?)

4. Felt versus unfelt needs. (Is there a pressing personal issue? Perhaps the disciple needs money or a job, and prayer for God's provision might supersede other activities.)

5. The specific prompting of the Spirit. (We have stated before that God is sovereign and reserves the right to lead us directly. For example, Philip left a burgeoning evangelism effort in Samaria to go to the desert and lead the Ethiopian to faith in Christ. Some commentaries attribute the African awakening to this event.)

Next, Prioritize Mark's Needs.

For Mark's Equipping *NGP* we prioritize the needs as follows:

- The need to learn to share his faith (See *NGP* Sample #1.)

- The need to have a more consistent devotional time (See *NGP* Sample #2.)

- The need to learn how to help a new believer begin to grow (See *NGP* Sample #3.)

Learning to share his faith (which includes sharing his testimony) is first because there is an evangelism training course offered that Mark needs to sign up for. Also, we see that Mark checked item #48 ("I am deeply concerned about people dying without knowing Christ.") on the Equipping portion, and this shows that Mark's heart is ready to reach out to others in the name of Christ.

Having a more consistent devotional time (which will be worked on at the same time as Need #1) is listed as #2 because of its critical importance in the life of a believer, especially one

---

[10] http://www.disciplebuilding.org/ministries/restorative-ministry/

who is having a ministry.

For Mark's Restorative *NGP* we prioritize the needs as follows:

- The need to "get in touch" with his emotions—to recognize, understand, and express (See *NGP* Sample #4 on page 94.)

- The need to face and deal with his addiction to work

- The need to learn how to set boundaries with other people (say "no")

Learning to recognize, understand and express his emotions is a foundational need that comes first. A person cannot effectively overcome an addiction until he is willing to deal with his emotions. Emotional health is a pre-requisite to relational health (setting boundaries).

Step 3: Set Goals Based on the Needs

After identifying a set of needs, define specific, measurable goals for meeting these needs. A goal is a specific target activity. For Susie, the need was rest; the goal was to get Susie to go to sleep. Not all goals are this simple to explain or set. The more we understand the type of need, the easier it is to write goals that are achievable and measurable. By narrowing the parameters of the needs, it is easier to write goals that match these needs.

Another way of thinking about this is to ask questions about the needs we observe using four specific categories:

1. Is there something this person needs to **know?**

2. Is there an **attitude** that needs to change?

3. Is there a **behavior** that needs to change?

4. Is there a particular **skill** this person needs to learn?

Using these categories helps our goals be more directed and specific. (You may have already realized how much we like the acronym as a tool for remem-

bering the various dimensions of disciple building. Well, here comes another one!) These categories are easier to remember by thinking of "KABS" (Knowledge, Attitude, Behavior, Skills). Being able to rough-sort a need into one or more of these categories can be very helpful and can prevent wasted effort and costly mistakes. This is a helpful general approach to needs, but there are noteworthy exceptions.

When a person has experienced some type of past emotional injury, there are complicating factors that affect attitudes and behavior. (For example, people who have been sexually abused by an adult will find it very difficult to trust any authority figure until some emotional healing has taken place.)

Let's make this practical: We discover that our disciple has an unfelt need to practice evangelism. (Think "KABS.") We might address this need by setting the goal of having her learn evangelism skills, if it were only an issue of learning a skill (Skill: "S"). We might set a teaching goal if the need was linked to knowing the biblical importance of evangelism (Knowledge: "K"). If our disciple has a problem with fear of failure (Attitude: "A"), we might establish overcoming fear as a goal. Sometimes what is most needed is simply to do what needs to be done (Behavior: "B"). Or the need may require goals in two or more of these areas: Knowledge, Attitude, Behavior, Skill.

Several times we have used the words "specific" and "measurable" when referring to goals. It is important that a goal focus on one subject and be measured quantitatively. For example, "attend an evangelism training conference this fall" focuses on one subject and can be measured ("Did the disciple attend such a conference?"). On the other hand, the goal "grow in his relationship with God," while an admirable goal, is too broad and cannot be measured quantitatively. As you look over the goals on the *NGP*s of Exhibit F on page 85, notice that they are specific and measurable.

Taking the time to think relationally helps us set better goals and begins to move us toward planning projects. Some needs are complex and involve setting goals in two or more areas simultaneously. Being sensitive to the Spirit of God and logging many hours of prayer will prove beneficial.

Step 4: Design Personal Growth Projects

Projects and plans are the specific activities that are designed to accomplish your goals. If learning evangelism skills is the goal, the project might be to have the disciple attend a weekend evangelism conference or go on an evangelistic outreach or visitation with your church. As you begin writing projects to implement your goals, it is helpful to look at the different things Jesus did with His disciples. The *R-CAPS Grid* is designed to help us identify and then plan around the five specific activities/responsibilities of a Life Coach.

The plans we make for our disciple should include at least one of these elements. For example, if the need is for a disciple to walk more intimately with God, the goal might be that the disciple establishes the discipline of a daily quiet time (a behavior), and the project/plan might look like this:

- **Relate (R)**

  The Life Coach continues to build a friendship relationship, showing love and concern by calling weekly, meeting bi-weekly and doing a fun activity once a month. The Life Coach shares about her personal quiet time, including struggles in getting started. The Life Coach models this by being consistent in her own quiet time.

- **Teach Content (C)**

  In a small group, the Life Coach teaches about the importance of a quiet time and the how to's. Since a part of teaching is training, the Life Coach shares a quiet time booklet with the disciple, demonstrating the use of

the how to's. (Use WDA's Laying Foundations, Small Group Study #1 in *Knowing God*.)

- **Hold Accountable (A)**

  The Life Coach asks the disciple specific questions about what she is learning and how God is helping her apply truth in her life.

- **Pray (P)**

  The Life Coach prays daily that the disciple will have desire and discipline.

- **Provide Growth Situations (S)**

  The Life Coach challenges the disciple with a specific and measurable goal of a 15-minute quiet time once a day.

The Spirit will give creative insight into the best approaches in each of these categories. The more familiar the Life Coach is with a variety of resources, the more effective she will become at designing projects/plans. See more *NGP* samples in Exhibit F of this manual.

Step 5: Evaluate and Update the Plan and Projects

It is easy to become wrapped up in planning and doing and fail to evaluate. However, lack of evaluation may eventually lead to ineffectiveness because mistakes are repeated rather than corrected. Evaluation also encourages thinking and creativity.

Use the following questions for evaluation:

- Were all the plans completed?

- Which were not? Why weren't they?

- What important information was gained about the disciple?

- Were the goals accomplished? Why or why not?

- Do I need to do something differently? Why? If so, what is my plan for doing it differently?

Concluding Thoughts on *NGP*s

Designing disciple building strategies (*NGP*s) is a learned skill that integrates wisdom principles gathered from careful study of the Scriptures with a sensitive dependence on the Holy Spirit. The Holy Spirit gives the wisdom to specifically apply truth at the right time and in the right way. Adopting the right method of administering truth is very important. Insulin is a life-saving medication for the diabetic. But how it is administered is equally important. Topical application has no effect. Only an injection of the right amount at the right time will prove effective. Similarly, the way we deliver truth is critical. Truth that is presented in an abrupt, uncaring manner is often not received. The truth remains true, but the recipient is unable to process it correctly. Scripture admonishes us to be sensitive and wise as we urge our disciples to apply the truth of God in their lives.

The *NGP* approach can be stilted, even legalistic, if the Life Coach ceases to maintain a humble dependence on the sovereign Lord and a deep respect for the person he is trying to help. Scripture teaches that we are fearfully and wonderfully made. This is true of our physical bodies, and it is also true of our unique personalities. We need to approach everyone as unique in Christ, and look to Him to help us help others.

Glossary	
RCAPS	Relationships, Content, Accountability, Prayer, Situations
NGP	Needs, Goals, Plans/Projects
CGC	Christian Growth Checklist
OPSI	Observation, Participation, Supervision, Independence
KABS	Knowledge, Attitude, Behavior, Skill

Life Coaching Appointments

The one-to-one personal appointment time is just one part of the relationship between a disciple and Life Coach, but it is a very important part. This section focuses on the elements of a one-to-one appointment and how to plan and evaluate appointments.

Checklist for a One-to-One Appointment

A common question asked about one-to-one Life Coaching appointments is: "What do we do in an appointment?" The ultimate answer to this question is: "It depends." It depends on the disciple, the circumstance, the felt needs present, and, of course, the leading of the Holy Spirit. This is why planning a one-to-one appointment is paramount. But before we address that, here is a list of possible elements to include in a one-to-one appointment.

1. Check on the disciple's personal walk with God.

Since the goal of every disciple is to grow into the likeness of Christ, a consistent interaction with God is essential. If this area is weak, all other areas will be affected.

Suggested questions:

- What has God been teaching you?

- How have your times with God been?

- What are the specific areas where you think

you need to grow?

2. Do non-ministry things together—have fun, share daily life activities.

The goal here is for the disciple to have a proper view of a balanced Christian life. It also gives the disciple an example of Christian behavior and attitudes in daily life situations.

Ask yourself:

- What common interests do we have?

- What interests (skills) do I have that I can share (and vice versa)?

- What daily activity can we share?

3. Share personal information:

- Share yourself, be transparent (joys, struggles, what God is teaching, felt needs, prayer requests, application of truth).

- Talk about life activities (school, family, etc.).

- Minister/counsel regarding felt needs.

- Goals: to be an example, to give a realistic view of the Christian life, to demonstrate love and interest, to build relationships.

4. Discuss the application of truth.

Since the Great Commission says to "teach them to observe all things," application of truth is essential to the life of a growing disciple. Suggestions:

- Ask yourself: What situations has the disciple been encountering in everyday life that may need special attention? How can I help him apply the truth of Scripture to these situations?

- Ask yourself: What truths has the disciple been taught in a small group/a large group?

- Then ask the disciple how one of these truths has affected his life. (Be more specific, if necessary.)

- If application questions were suggested with the truth, use them with the disciple.

5. Discuss accountability issues.

Accountability can be a controversial topic. For some, accountability can mean a system of legalistic (even abusive) control where every area of a disciple's life is open to the nit-picking gaze of the disciple builder/Life Coach. For others, accountability is limited only to the areas in which a disciple "feels comfortable discussing the topics." These extremes need to be avoided. We advocate a more balanced approach where boundaries are respected when areas of need are strategically pinpointed. For this to occur, you need an overarching plan that the disciple and the Life Coach can agree on and support. The *NGP* approach accomplishes this goal. Discussion is limited to areas where both Life Coach and disciple recognize needs. If other needs emerge, the Life Coach is able to point out areas where there may need to be further work. This is not always comfortable for either party, but it leads to productive growth.

- Explore together specific needs and areas of growth in the disciple's life that are linked to the *NGP* you have developed.

- If new areas emerge, discuss these, and if necessary, reprioritize the *NGP*.

- Remember the parameters of accountability. The privilege of holding a disciple accountable is given as a trust relationship is built. This cannot be rushed or forced.

Some ways of holding a disciple accountable are more helpful than others. Simply finding out if he was successful or unsuccessful in the area of accountability is usually not helpful because it may result in feelings of guilt and discouragement if he was unsuccessful. Instead, it is more effective to work with the disciple to develop a plan for dealing with the problem area and then hold him accountable to take the specific steps in his plan. While there may be successes and failures on specific steps of the plan, if the plan is well conceived, the disciple will overcome the problem in time.

6. Do ministry business.

There may be no ministry business at the beginning (Phases I and II). However, at later phases there will be: sharing faith, planning a small group, preparing a lesson, evaluating a lesson or group, doing administrative tasks, etc.

7. Pray together; share requests.

This is important to centering your relationship on Christ and for modelling.

8. Personal teaching.

This includes any direct teaching that needs to be done (a missed lesson reviewed, a felt need met, etc.). Pocket Principles® are useful here.

Planning a One-to-One Appointment

Time spent one-to-one with a disciple is important in the discipling process. It is essential to carefully think through and plan one-to-one appointments. Too often the content of personal time spent with a disciple is dictated by convenience and circumstance only. Planning one-to-one appointments does not mean they must be rigid times spent accomplishing a list of subjects/activities. (Remember that flexibility is an important quality in the disciple building relationship.) Planning means that you as the Life Coach have prayed about and thought through the needs of your disciple and have ideas and guidelines about how to meet those needs in a one-to-one appointment.

As you read the checklist material above, it undoubtedly became apparent that you cannot do every element at each appointment. These are merely suggested areas. YOU as the discipler/Life Coach must make decisions about what to cover. As you do so, it is helpful to consider these factors:

- Time available—What can realistically be done in the time you have? What should have priority if time is short?

- Balance—All of these elements are important and need to be included at one appointment or another. It is unwise to focus consistently on only one or two elements for a long period of time. Beware of doing only what is easiest.

- Felt needs—Obviously, if a felt need is domi-

nant in your disciple's mind and emotions, it needs to be dealt with before other needs can be focused on.

- Unfelt needs—These will vary according to the individual and the Phase of the disciple's growth.

As you plan a one-to-one appointment, ask the Holy Spirit to guide you and give you wisdom and discernment regarding needs and how to meet them. Then, taking these factors into consideration, establish a plan, including one or more of the seven elements. As you plan, write down what you want to accomplish (goals) and how you will proceed (projects).

Example A:

Goal: To see that the principles of a Christian lifestyle pervade all of life.

Project: Ask disciple to go with you to the mall and shop for a birthday gift. Go to the grocery store. Then cook and eat dinner together at home.

Example B:

Goal: To recognize ways Jesus has met needs in the disciple's life (follow-up of a small group study in John on Jesus as the One who meets our needs).

Project: Review truths taught in lesson. Ask disciple questions to stimulate thinking: What needs have you seen God meet recently in your life? What is one particular need you have that you want God to meet? How can we pray about that? You share a need you have. Pray together about the specific need. Be faithful to follow-up on prayer request.

Evaluating a One-to-One Appointment

After your appointment it is important to evaluate. Ask yourself:

- Were goals accomplished? Why or why not?

- Should I have done anything differently?

- Based on the results of this appointment, are

there specific things I need to do in the next appointment? in this disciple's small group study? in my personal ministry?

Careful evaluation will keep you from continuing to make the same errors. Also, if you think about the next appointment as you evaluate the previous one, it will help the content of your one-to-one appointments flow in a meaningful way.

It is important to keep a *written record* of the appointment plans and evaluations. As you have more and more one-to-one appointments you will discover that they begin to blur together and the details become fuzzy. Keeping a written record is the only way to assure clarity and accuracy.

Common Life Coach Problem Areas

Program Orientation instead of Relationship Orientation

Because we are attempting to integrate relationships with a disciple building program, there may be the temptation to view a relationship from a strictly utilitarian viewpoint—to view a relationship as a means of furthering the program rather than as valuable in itself. You may find yourself focusing on getting your disciple into Equipping for Ministry rather than developing her character. To avoid this danger be sure that love is your central motivation and that you keep in mind the goal of Christ-likeness. God's love and power at work within you will provide this motivation. Careful attention to this area and earnest prayer are essential.

Lack of Natural Affinity

Another danger in the area of relationships and disciple building is to allow natural affinity (or the lack of it) to have an inappropriate influence. A natural affinity with a disciple is a gift; however, that affinity should not cause you to be irresponsible to other disciples or to show favoritism. On the other hand, if natural affinity is missing you need not feel guilty or inadequate but instead should endeavor to be faithful to your disciple; pray that God will knit your hearts together and look for areas of common interest. Learning to work at a re-

lationship that does not come easily can be a valuable experience for both you and your disciple.

Moving Too Fast

Building a relationship is a slow process. Give your Life Coaching relationships the time and space they need to develop naturally. Be aware of the danger of pushing a relationship, such as trying to get too deep too fast. Since trust and voluntary account-ability are essential to disciple building, moving too fast can thwart the process.

Giving Up Too Easily

Because of personality differences, natural affinity (or lack of it), external circumstances, etc., relationships develop at different speeds. Be patient. Wise, loving perseverance will have its reward.

Taking Too Much Responsibility

Beware of the temptation to become overly responsible for your disciple. Your disciple is a child of God, with a will of his own, who is responsible directly to God. You as the Life Coach are to serve as an encourager, catalyst, rebuker, teacher, modeler, etc., but you are NOT responsible for your disciple's choices, actions and words. It is easy to fall into this way of thinking. Keeping your focus on God and your call to obedience to Him is important.

Lacking a Sense of Direction

It is easy to meet with and relate to a disciple without encouraging that disciple to grow. This happens when you as a Life Coach have not thought about and prayed through needs, goals and plans for the disciple. Careful planning and evaluation will help you avoid a relationship in which the disciple is not challenged to grow.

Only Relating on a Spiritual Level

Another danger is to focus your relationship with your disciple only on spiritual issues, ignoring mental, emotional, social and physical needs and goals. God created us as whole people, and growing in Christlikeness involves every area of our lives. Again, careful, thoughtful planning and evaluation will help you avoid this pitfall.

Life Coaching Recommendations

Make wise choices regarding your time.

Let's face it. One of the biggest challenges to disciple building involves the scheduling demands of Life Coaching someone. Most people lead busy lives with few spare moments for adding another appointment to the day-planner. Scripture admonishes us, "be very careful, then, how you live, not as unwise but as wise, making the most of every opportunity, because the days are evil. Therefore do not be foolish, but understand what the Lord's will is." (Ephesians 5:15-17)

Disciple building requires wisdom, especially in managing our time. Weary, burned-out Life Coaches have little to offer others. There is not an exact science for scheduling appointments with disciples, nor is there a formula or ideal structure for organizing a tiered approach to disciple building. But there are principles that can help guide us. It becomes the responsibility of each Life Coach to seek and discover the best configuration for her. In fact, the very process of grappling with the issue of timing and scheduling forces us to seek God's will revealed through the Spirit. This in turn causes us to grow as leaders. "It is the glory of God to conceal a matter, but the glory of kings is to search out a matter."(NAS) This is hard work, but it's part of the process, and it's worth the effort!

Use real life experiences.

Some of the very best moments in Life Coaching occur naturally, in the course of everyday events. Life must be lived by running errands, shopping, transporting children, working in the yard and waiting in traffic. Whenever possible, ask your disciple to hang out with you in real time, in real life. Run errands together, go to the movies, watch a game, wash the car. This was the primary teaching approach of Jesus and the Old Testament Patriarchs. Jesus invited His disciples to come with Him and travel with Him on mission projects. The Law was to be communicated "when you sit at home and when you walk along the road, when you lie down and when you get up." It is in the course of everyday life that the best teaching moments occur. This requires some planning and making the most of opportunities. It also reflects a willingness to allow our disciples to see us not just when we have a prearranged curriculum, but when the phone is ringing and the bathtub is overflowing. This requires transparency and humility, and it has great value. Modelling truth is one of the best ways of communicating truth.

Use the existing time slots of your local church.

Look for ways that you can coordinate with your local church leaders to facilitate a disciple building approach. A Sunday School class is a great place to teach many of the principles of disciple building, especially if you are able to meet with members outside of class. If home fellowship groups already exist as part of the structure, volunteer to lead one.[11] Many churches offer a mid-week training class. Offer to teach some of the progressive principles/theology during these time slots.[12] Most churches already have established ministry teams such as evangelistic outreach or commu-

[11] For more information about how to conduct progressive disciple building small groups, see *Small Groups Manual* (WDA).

[12] The WDA Disciple Building Teaching Outlines are designed for use by the leader in a classroom.

nity assistance programs. If you are helping disciples at the phase of Equipping for Ministry, don't "reinvent the wheel" by trying to create ministry opportunities; instead look for ways you can partner with the leadership of these teams. Besides saving time and effort, it also capitalizes on the dynamic of body-life and builds unity.

Use the 1/1/2-4 configuration.

Our experience in helping lay people make disciples has taught us that few people can Life Coach more than four people at once. Most can only coach two. We can achieve biblical reproduction and multiplication if we faithfully disciple only two who can (in turn) disciple two others, etc. But while we're helping others grow we must not forget that we also need encouragement and accountability. If practical, we need a Life Coach and a ministry partner who can encourage us. We need someone over us, someone beside us, and two to four others that we are helping to grow. This is the ideal configuration for the "geom-

etry" of disciple building. It also helps to establish a larger movement. We refer to this configuration as: 1/1/2-4. A better way to understand it is by looking at the diagram below:

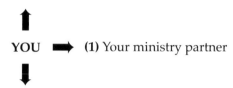

(1) The person Life Coaching you

YOU ➡ **(1)** Your ministry partner

(2-4) Two to four people you're coaching

In this configuration we are relating to others at three different levels of Christian maturity. We are coaching two to four others who are less mature, we are growing alongside a ministry partner who is roughly at the same point of maturity that we are. We are looking to an older, more mature, leader for wisdom and guidance.

Conclusion

We began this manual by identifying Jesus as the ultimate Life Coach. In the Great Commission He gave His disciples, the ones that walked with Him on this earth and those of us who walk with Him now by the power of the Holy Spirit, the command to build disciples (Matthew 28:18-20). Part of building disciples is teaching and influencing them by the strength of example and modelling. This influence depends on having a strong, healthy relationship between the disciple and Life Coach. This manual has presented instructions, principles and advice about building a Life Coach relationship with a disciple. But, ultimately, a manual is only words on paper. The final test of these instructions, principles and advice is in the real life relationships that are built in the midst of day-to-day struggles, busyness and distractions.

It is possible to become familiar with the content

> It is only as you enter the fray and start building disciples that you will ultimately learn how to build disciples.

of this manual and never become familiar with the practice of building disciples. It is only as you enter the fray and start building disciples that you will ultimately learn how to build disciples. A student pilot spends hours in "ground school" studying principles of aerodynamics and flying techniques. But it is only as he flies the actual airplane that he really learns to fly. In a similar way, it is impossible to fully learn about building disciples without actually meeting with and relating to a disciple, prayerfully designing *NGPs*, and carrying out growth projects with the goal of helping a disciple grow into Christlikeness.

So, go and do it! You will make mistakes. But as you struggle you will learn and grow. Remember, He promised to use His great authority to support you, and He also promised, "Surely I am with you always, to the very end of the age." Blessings!

Exhibit A:

What Jesus Did – What We Can Do

Phase I: Establishing Faith

Primary Goal: To reach out to unbelievers and proclaim the Gospel in an effort to establish faith in Christ alone for salvation, and conduct basic follow-up with new Christians.

What Jesus Did		What We Can Do
Jesus and John the Baptist: •Went to the lost sheep of Israel and showed concern and care for their spiritual condition by delivering a tough message, laced with love •Gathered people who needed to hear the message and those who had responded to the message *Isaiah 40:3 cf. 42:3/Matthew 9:12 "I have come to call sinners."*	**Relationships**	•Build relationships with unbelievers in an attempt to "connect"
•Taught God's love, holiness, the atonement of the Lamb of God, the future judgment, the role of the Holy Spirit, evangelistic apologetics, and the divine nature of Christ *John 1:29-34 "Behold the Lamb of God who takes away the sin of the world."*	**Content**	•Share with unbelievers the Good News and answer their questions about the Christian faith •Follow up with those who respond
•Called people to repent, turn away from contemporary idols and put their trust in God's deliverer (Messiah) •Exhorted the people to become followers (disciples) of this Promised One *Matthew 3:1-2 "Repent, for the Kingdom of Heaven is near."*	**Accountability**	•Challenge people to repent, accept Christ and publicly declare their faith in Him
•Asked God to call men to become Christ's disciples •Asked that the strong man would be bound and the power of the enemy broken so the Word might be proclaimed *Matthew 16:19 "Whatever you bind on earth will be bound in heaven."*	**Prayer**	•Pray for opportunities to share Christ with unbelievers •Pray and prepare for the spiritual attacks •Pray that people will become aware of their own emotional needs
•Had various evangelistic encounters and situations where relationships could be established •Had large groups, small groups (in homes and at public gatherings) and individual contacts *Matthew 9:10 "While Jesus was having dinner at Matthew's house, many tax collectors and sinners came and ate with Him and His disciples."*	**Situations**	•Conduct evangelistic outreaches in communities •Hold evangelistic socials in our homes and churches •Provide opportunities for new disciples to publicly confess their faith in Christ

©WDA 1997-2015

Scriptures from The Harmony of the Gospels:
Matthew 3:1 - 4:11; Mark 1:1-13; Luke 2:1-2, 3:3-18,21-23, 4:1-13; John 1:19-28

Phase II: Laying Foundations

Primary Goal: To gather young believers into a small group to help them understand the foundational truths of the Christian life and involve them in the larger Christian community.

What Jesus Did		What We Can Do
•Challenged a group of disciples to be with Him •Spent time with them individually and as a group •Revealed His identity as Messiah *John 1:39 "Rabbi, where are you staying?" "Come and you will see!"*	**Relationships**	•Gather an "open" group of young believers who desire to grow •Begin spending time getting to know each of them •Create an honest, safe, grace-oriented, sharing environment that facilitates trust & emotional safety
•Revealed Himself to them as the Messiah through His teaching and miracles •Taught that the Kingdom of God under Messianic rule had appeared and that God had provided an opportunity for them to participate *John 2:11 "He thus revealed His glory, and His disciples put their faith in Him."*	**Content**	•Teach new disciples the "foundational truths" of the Christian life: The person and work of Christ, the ministry of the Holy Spirit, the sovereign plan of God, and how to grow spiritually
•Challenged them to put their faith fully in Him as their Teacher and Guide •Challenged some to become His followers *John 1:43 "Finding Phillip He said to him, 'Follow me.'"*	**Accountability**	•Challenge them to be committed to learning how to grow by having a Quiet Time and being around other believers •Invite them to participate in a small group •Encourage them to share emotions & needs •Identify emotional trauma & faulty belief systems •Encourage them to look to God to meet their needs in answer to their specific prayers
• Asked God the Father to call men to follow Him and reveal that He was the Christ •Prayed that power would be made available to accomplish attesting miracles *John 1:47ff. (to Nathaniel) "I saw you when you were under the fig tree...you shall see...angels ascending and descending on the Son of Man."*	**Prayer**	•Ask God to reveal Himself to these new disciples in powerful and intimate ways, answering their prayers and helping them gain insights into His nature and power
•Performed miracles attesting to His divine nature and authority •Set up various teaching situations both publicly and privately •Established His Messianic authority over Israel by cleansing the Temple •Formed a group of followers and took them with Him as He taught and performed miracles *John 3:2 (Nicodemus) "Rabbi, no one could perform the miraculous signs you are doing if God were not with him!"*	**Situations**	•Provide opportunities for new followers to become involved in the Christian community by delegating logistical tasks •Provide social functions to establish relationships with more mature believers •Assign an accountability partner •Be prepared for the Lord to precipitate specific needs that He will provide for

Scriptures from The Harmony of the Gospels:
Matthew 4:12-17; Mark 1:14-15; Luke 3:19-20, 4:14-31; John 1:29 - 4:54

Phase III: Equipping for Ministry

Primary Goal: To equip the disciples for ministry in the Kingdom and learn more about the nature of the Kingdom and the principles which govern their role as citizens who are sons and daughters.

What Jesus Did

What We Can Do

Relationships

•Challenged a few of His disciples to participate in His mission of winning the souls of people •Allowed them to follow Him into spiritual battles and observe His power and authority •Trained them as apprentices working alongside a Master

Mark 1:16ff. "He saw Simon and his brother Andrew casting a net into the sea…and said to them, 'Come, follow Me, and I will send you out to fish for people.'"

•Encourage our disciples to be with us as we model a ministry lifestyle •Model healthy relationships •Set & respect boundaries •Be willing to confront others in a caring way •Maintain priorities, and model other aspects of healthy relationships

Content

•Stressed the importance of telling others about His mission and love for sinners •Trained them in basic ministry skills •Gave them insights into the nature of His Kingdom: He was Conqueror over the kingdom of darkness; had authority to forgive sin, heal sickness, and dispel demons

Luke 5:23ff. "Which is easier to say, 'Your sins are forgiven….'?"

•Offer training in evangelism skills •Teach about the sovereign authority of Christ over the spiritual realm and the traditions of men •Review the truths of the Gospel with the purpose of helping others understand •Teach and model healthy relationships •Teach about positional truth

Accountability

•Called His disciples to be fishers of men •Challenged them to leave their worldly pursuits (at least temporarily) and follow Him on mission

Matthew 4:20 "At once they left their nets and followed Him."

•Challenge people to go with us as we reach out to the lost in our community •Challenge them to get training in how to win others to Christ •Encourage them to participate in various ministry situations •Construct projects that address emotional/spiritual strongholds

Prayer

•Prayed for healing power and deliverance for those trapped in sin and satanic strongholds •Asked for their eyes to be opened to see and understand the spiritual battles raging around them •Prayed for another generation of disciples to repent and follow Him

II Kings 6 (Elisha's servant) cf. Matthew 16:13-19

•Ask God to open doors for our disciples to share their faith •Pray God would give them a vision and burden for the lost •Ask God to free them from emotional and relational bondage

Situations

•Took His disciples on a short-term mission project to upper Galilee •Challenged the status quo of religious traditions and human philosophies •Healed the sick and cast out demons

Matthew 4:23 "Jesus went throughout Galilee, teaching in their Synagogues, preaching the Good News of the Kingdom, and healing every disease and sickness."
John 3:2 (Nicodemus) "Rabbi…no one could perform the miraculous signs you are doing if God were not with him!"

•Take our disciples with us as we minister •Make time to debrief after our ministry times together •Offer opportunities to focus on ministry events, thus showing a willingness to change traditions for the sake of extending the Kingdom (retreats, concerts of prayer, evangelism training, mission projects, restorative opportunities, etc)

Scriptures from The Harmony of the Gospels:
Matthew 4:13-25, 8:2-4,14-17, 9:1-17, 12:1-21; Mark 1:16 - 3:12; Luke 4:31 - 6:11; John 5:1-47

Phase IV: Developing New Leaders

Primary Goal: To appoint a group of leaders and train them to apply kingdom principles as they assist in the ministry and help others grow.

What Jesus Did		What We Can Do
•Appointed the Twelve to be with Him as leaders in His ministry •Allowed them to assume important ministry roles and gave them authority •Sent them out in pairs to preach and minister in His Name •Spent extra time instructing them as a group and individually *Luke 6:13 "He called His disciples to Him and chose twelve of them."*	**Relationships**	•Appoint leaders •Train leaders as they assume roles of responsibility in the overall ministry and over individuals •Be prepared to provide encouraging perspective when God challenges their status quo
•Taught the principles of Kingdom life as being distinct from religious traditions •Explained that true religion was from the heart and not merely external acts •Taught the eternal nature of God's plan and purpose and the wisdom of placing priority on eternal over temporal matters •Taught principles of spiritual authority and warfare *Matthew 5-7 (Sermon on the Mount)*	**Content**	•Teach basic leadership skills •Explain that true discipleship will produce Christlikeness and that biblical ministry involves growth in character, not just success in ministry programs •Teach about spiritual warfare, problem solving, team dynamics and how to resolve conflict
•Challenged their human propensity to put their trust in themselves and the temporal systems of men •Tested them by disrupting their life and ministry •Jeopardized the success of His public ministry to emphasize the importance of internal obedience, faith, and eternal priorities *John 6:5 "Where shall we buy bread for these people to eat?"*	**Accountability**	•Allow our disciples to fail •Challenge them to assume responsibility in ministry tasks that appear bigger than their abilities •Help them rearrange their priorities around their new responsibilities
•Prayed that God would give wisdom in selecting the disciples who were ready for leadership •Asked that they might see the greatness of God and their own insufficiency and that God would provide supernaturally *Luke 6:12 "Jesus went out to a mountainside to pray, and spent the night praying to God. When morning came...."*	**Prayer**	•Pray for wisdom in the leadership selection process •Ask that they might see the greatness of God and their own insufficiency •Ask God to provide for them supernaturally
•Gave them real responsibilities in His ministry •Set up ministry situations that required supernatural provision and demanded faith •Created a new structure in His ministry: the Leadership Team which allowed Him opportunities to apply truth at a deeper level by instructing these leaders separately from the main body of disciples and/or the interested others •Required them to spend more time with Him and the work, thus causing them to reevaluate their priorities *John 6 "Do not work for the food which perishes, but...endures."*	**Situations**	•Help them develop the gifts God has given them by positioning them in roles that suit them •Send them into situations that will be sure to invite spiritual warfare •Give them responsibilities to disciple and mentor young believers •Include them in the Leadership Team

©WDA 1997-2015

Scriptures from The Harmony of the Gospels:
Matthew 5:1 - 17:23; Mark 3:13 - 9:32; Luke 6:12 - 9:45; John 6:1 - 7:1

Phase V: Developing Mature Leaders

Primary Goal: To develop a group of mature disciples who have a vision for reaching the nations through God's enabling power, and to have an ability to make other disciples according to the pattern Jesus used.

What Jesus Did | | ## What We Can Do

What Jesus Did		What We Can Do
•Reduced their dependence on him while continuing to have an intimate relationship with them by giving them more independence and slowly weaning them from Himself •Challenged them to be committed to one another •Washed their feet •Laid down His life on the Cross *John 15:15-17 "I have called you friends, for everything that I learned from My Father I have made known to you. ...Love each other."*	**Relationships**	•Focus our training and attention on our disciples' full development •Commission them as peers in ministry •Continue to serve and love them as friends
•Taught the importance of reaching all the nations, the all-sufficiency of the Spirit, the inadequacy of human strength, the importance of unity in the Body, how the church should function and how to demonstrate agape love in the midst of relational struggles *John 17:23 "May they be brought to complete unity to let the world know that you sent me...."*	**Content**	•Teach the importance of unity, reaching the nations, suffering love, and (advanced) leadership skills •Teach the dynamics of family life and church life •Remind them that though they have been trained, discipleship is never fully completed until we stand before Christ
•Challenged them to love one another •Commanded them to feed and care for His sheep •Challenged them to go into the entire world and make disciples *John 15:17 "This is my command: Love each other."*	**Accountability**	•Challenge them to consider what worldwide mission involvement would look like for them •Exhort them to set aside petty differences and strive to put each other first •Suggest they become less dependent on us as mentors and form new ministry relationships
•Prayed they would be able to overcome the enemy and their fleshly self-sufficiency •Asked that they would experience the fullness and enabling of the Holy Spirit *Luke 22:31 "Simon, Simon, Satan has asked to sift you like wheat. But I have prayed for you."*	**Prayer**	•Pray God would allow them to humbly rest in the power of Christ's Spirit in them •Ask for unity and love to prevail as the enemy puts stress on re-lationships •Ask God to give them a vision and burden for the entire world
•Gave them increased responsibility in leading the ministry •Moved His ministry beyond the borders of Palestine •Commanded them to go into the entire world to make disciples and then teach these disciples to put into practice the same things they had been taught *Matthew 28:18-20 "Go and make disciples of all nations...."*	**Situations**	•Include them as part of a leadership team that directs the larger ministry •Take the Great Commission seriously by setting up discipleship training and world missions opportunities •Watch for the Lord to put our disciples, and us, in situations where they/we are incapable of pulling ministry off in our own strength

Scriptures from The Harmony of the Gospels:
Matthew 17:24 - 28:20; Mark 9:33 - 16:20; Luke 9:46 - 24:53; John 7:2 - 21:25; Acts 1:1 - 2:4

Exhibit B:

The R-CAPS Grid And Legend

The R-CAPS Grid:
Strategy for the Disciple Builder

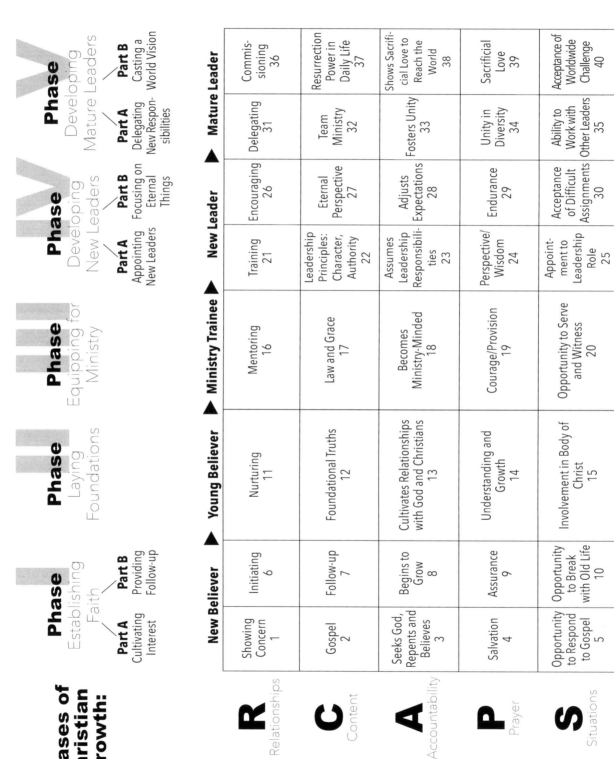

Phases of Christian Growth:

- **Phase I** — Establishing Faith: **Part A** Cultivating Interest, **Part B** Providing Follow-up
- **Phase II** — Laying Foundations
- **Phase III** — Equipping for Ministry
- **Phase IV** — Developing New Leaders: **Part A** Appointing New Leaders, **Part B** Focusing on Eternal Things; Developing Mature Leaders: **Part A** Delegating New Responsibilities, **Part B** Casting a World Vision

	New Believer (Part A)	New Believer (Part B)	Young Believer	Ministry Trainee	New Leader (Part A)	New Leader (Part B)	Mature Leader (Part A)	Mature Leader (Part B)
R (Relationships)	Showing Concern 1	Initiating 6	Nurturing 11	Mentoring 16	Training 21	Encouraging 26	Delegating 31	Commissioning 36
C (Content)	Gospel 2	Follow-up 7	Foundational Truths 12	Law and Grace 17	Leadership Principles: Character, Authority 22	Eternal Perspective 27	Team Ministry 32	Resurrection Power in Daily Life 37
A (Accountability)	Seeks God, Repents and Believes 3	Begins to Grow 8	Cultivates Relationships with God and Christians 13	Becomes Ministry-Minded 18	Assumes Leadership Responsibilities 23	Adjusts Expectations 28	Fosters Unity 33	Shows Sacrificial Love to Reach the World 38
P (Prayer)	Salvation 4	Assurance 9	Understanding and Growth 14	Courage/Provision 19	Perspective/Wisdom 24	Endurance 29	Unity in Diversity 34	Sacrificial Love 39
S (Situations)	Opportunity to Respond to Gospel 5	Opportunity to Break with Old Life 10	Involvement in Body of Christ 15	Opportunity to Serve and Witness 20	Appointment to Leadership Role 25	Acceptance of Difficult Assignments 30	Ability to Work with Other Leaders 35	Acceptance of Worldwide Challenge 40

The R-CAPS Legend:
Strategy for the Disciple Builder

Phase I: Establishing Faith

Part A — Cultivating Interest

Showing Concern (R) Disciple Builder:

1a   Goes into unbeliever's world: relates in casual, social situations; develops friendships with those who are open; shows compassion; meets felt needs.

1b   Invites those who are curious to get together in groups.

1c   Is transparent about his beliefs in the normal course of conversation. Doesn't hide who he is, but also doesn't press his views.

Disciple Builder: The goal here is to show unbelievers the love of Christ. You should enter into their world and show love, compassion and genuine interest. Show them in practical ways that the love of Jesus is relevant and sufficient to meet their needs. Also, be available to answer questions.

Gospel (C) Disciple Builder:

2a   Addresses felt needs from a biblical perspective: relationships, self-esteem, career, etc. as a way of showing God's love and holiness.

2b   Answers questions and objections (apologetics).

2c   Presents plan of salvation: e.g., God's justice, wrath, judgment, love, mercy, grace and forgiveness; Christ's substitution; and our need for genuine repentance and faith.

Disciple Builder: It's important to focus on meeting a person's felt needs — areas he wants help in (marriage, parenting, finances, etc.). Address these from a biblical perspective as interest and the relationship allow. That is, if the person is somewhat hostile to spiritual issues, you might not directly refer to what the Bible says about a particular issue. Be sensitive.

When a person is interested in spiritual things, the leader can introduce him to more biblical information. However, it is important that the leader be sure that this biblical information is presented in understandable, relevant terms (not Christian jargon that may be meaningless or overwhelming). The person needs to know the basics of God's character and how to become a Christian. You as the leader need to discern what is holding the person back and plan appropriately. (For example, if it is a heart / willingness issue, you may need to pray and continue being a friend. If there is a specific issue hindering the person, you may need to help resolve that issue.)

Seeks God, Repents and Believes (A)
Unbeliever:

3a   Shows interest in knowing more about God (e.g., responds to an invitation to a Christian event).

3b   Begins to think about God and ask questions.

3c   Confesses, repents and puts faith in God (makes restitution, if necessary).

Disciple Builder: To become a believer, the person must repent and make a decision to follow Christ. His life will begin to change, and you will begin to see fruit. Do not rush this transition. Genuine repentance is essential to growth.

Salvation (P) Disciple Builder prays:

4a   For open doors, boldness and words to speak.

4b   For God to break down strongholds and build interest in unbeliever.

4c   For repentance and faith in God (for unbeliever to see sin, believe in God's judgment, understand God's message of repentance, understand and respond to God's love and forgiveness, gain respect for God and His Word, and for God to expose idols in the person's life).

Disciple Builder: Much of the work will be done by the Holy Spirit in the person's heart. Prayer is essential.

Opportunity to Respond to Gospel (S) Disciple Builder:

5a   Puts unbeliever or new Christian in situations in which he can experience God's love and character through Christians. For example: invites unbeliever to evangelistic Bible study (or meets one-to-one to discuss a study); invites to socials, etc. with Christians.

5b   Looks for situations in which disciple builder can help meet the person's needs.

Disciple Builder: Usually you will be with unbelievers or new Christians in daily situations of life (at the gym, dinner after work, a coffee break, a camping trip, etc.), not special religious events. Be sensitive to the person's level of interest and do not push him. Also, ask the person to help you with something (a household repair or another area he has expertise in). This willingness to ask for help demonstrates a humility that is attractive and builds the relationship. As a person becomes interested in spiritual things, you can be more direct by inviting him to Bible studies, etc. Again, however, you need to be careful not to overwhelm him with information or pressure him to make a commitment.

Part B — Providing Follow-Up

Initiating (R) Disciple Builder:

6a   Intentionally initiates with the new believer in order to begin the follow-up process.

6b   Continues to develop a casual friendship with new believer.

Follow-Up (C) Disciple Builder:

7a   Shares basic follow-up information: assurance of salvation, baptism, fellowship with other believers, importance of the Word, basics of prayer and Bible study.

7b   Teaches benefits of following Christ: fellowship in Christ, eternal security in Christ.

Disciple Builder: These are the truths that form the basis of the life and growth of a Christian. The author of Hebrews refers to the "elementary teachings" in Hebrews 6:1. Understanding and beginning to live these truths is essential since Christlikeness is the goal.

Begins to Grow (A) New Believer:

8a   Begins to grow: associates with other Christians, grows in assurance in relationship with Christ, takes steps to learn more.

8b   Begins to practice repentance daily (life begins to change); demonstrates humility.

8c   Publicly identifies with Christ and His body (through baptism).

Disciple Builder: At this point, you will begin to see changes in the new believer's life. It is difficult to list specific changes to look for because they vary based on the person's need and the sovereign choice of God. However, the changes will occur primarily in the areas of attitude toward God and others. Some "sin" areas (especially habits that are deeply ingrained) may remain because the new believer is still quite young in his relationship with God. Be careful not to expect too much too soon or to impose legalistic standards. The person is ready to move on to Phase II: Laying Foundations when he understands and has begun to practice the follow-up truths.

Assurance (I') Disciple Builder prays:

9a   For protection as the Gospel takes hold.

9b   For a teachable heart.

9c   For new believer to be in situations in which he can see God at work in and for him.

9d   For new believer to understand the assurance of his salvation, his eternal security, the fact that God loves him, the forgiveness of his sins, the fact that the Holy Spirit dwells in him, that the Bible is the Word of God.

Disciple Builder: Many ingredients go into the new Christian's growth in his new life in Christ: enjoying fellowship with other Christians, becoming acquainted with the Bible, understanding what God has done in his life, getting to know Jesus, dealing with sin areas in his life, etc. Prayer is essential as the new believer and the disciple builder look to God as the source of growth.

Opportunity to Break with Old Life (S)
Disciple Builder:

10a   Invites new believer to attend a small group (or one-to-one appointments) for follow-up study.

10b   Looks for opportunities for the new believer to fellowship with Christians.

10c   Gives new believer the opportunity to confess his new faith in various situations.

Disciple Builder: It should not be expected that the new believer's testimony be smooth or technically perfect at this point in his development. (At Phase III: Equipping for Ministry, time will be spent sharing how to prepare a testimony.) The purpose of giving the new believer opportunities to talk about what God has done in his life (salvation) is to encourage him and solidify the commitment he has made.

Phase II: Laying Foundations

Nurturing (R) Disciple Builder:

11a   Begins leading an open and safe group (i.e., people may come and go) in which relationships can develop (informal; not a long-term personal commitment).

11b   Gives new disciple a chance to grow in love for and commitment to other believers.

11c   Continues to develop a trust relationship with disciple. Begins to model tasks (using the "steps of transfer" listed below) undertaken in the ministry (witnessing, sharing testimony). The relationship is casual, but disciple builder is available.

Disciple Builder: The term "steps of transfer" refers to the procedure used in training a disciple in a skill or activity. The steps of transfer are: Observation (O), Participation (P), Supervision (S), and Independence (I). Note that the abbreviation "OPSI" is used in this Legend. At the step of Observation, a disciple watches as the leader performs a task or activity. At the Participation step, he performs the task or activity with the leader. In the Supervision step, a disciple performs the task or activity alone, but with the supervision of the leader. At the last step of transfer, Independence, a disciple works on his own, independent of the disciple builder.

The commitment referred to in 11a and 11b is not an extensive, formal commitment, but a relational commitment. It is a commitment based on a personal relationship developed with Jesus, with the leader and with others in the small group. The "safe" atmosphere of the small group (mentioned in 11a) comes from the trust relationships built between the disciple and the leader and to a lesser extent between the disciple and other group members. The leader needs to create an atmosphere of grace – an environment in which there is an assurance of receiving love and where confidentiality is maintained so that there can be honesty about struggles and problems. As the leader gets to know the disciple, he will begin to see emotional and relational problems (if any). As trust develops, the leader can begin to gently expose them. If they are severe, he can help the disciple find help.

Foundational Truths (C) Disciple Builder:

12a   Teaches about the person and work of Christ: deity, authority, power, sovereignty, Lordship.

12b   Shares how to walk daily with Christ: importance of obedience, daily acceptance by grace, role and work of the Holy Spirit, spiritual disciplines, basic principles of divine guidance.

12c   Shows in Scripture that Christ is the intercessor and helper for all needs.

12d   Shares how to deal with emotions (past and present).

12e   Helps disciple develop a better understanding that God created people with needs and emotions.

Disciple Builder: The foundation of the rest of the disciple's Christian life is his personal relationship with Jesus. Therefore, it is important to go through content slowly enough for him to apply the truths he is learning. It is tempting to study material (information) and then go on to the next topic without waiting for God the Holy Spirit to use time and circumstances to make the truths real in daily life.

Regarding teaching on the Holy Spirit, the emphasis here should be on the role of the Spirit (as the source of power, the fruit of the Spirit, etc.) in the believer's growth process, not on the spiritual gifts.

Cultivates Relationships with God and Christians (A) Disciple:

13a   Is regularly involved with Christian activities: accepts small tasks within the body, seeks fellowship with Christians.

13b   Is committed to a small group Bible study, open to correction.

13c   Is developing a growing relationship with Jesus: is cultivating a daily quiet time (prayer, Bible study, Scripture memory, etc.), is seeking to walk obediently with Christ daily, is talking with others about Jesus and is growing in sensitivity to sin.

13d   Is developing an awareness of own emotional issues and is willing to work on them.

Disciple Builder: The definition of "committed" here means to attend faithfully, complete brief homework assignments and meet occasionally with the leader. Commitment at the beginning of the small group may be less than this; however, the disciple should be growing toward this commitment. At this point in the disciple's growth, the leader should be available to answer questions and help with faith steps, but not crowd the disciple or try to force growth. Be careful not to require (expect) too much commitment too soon. Your level of commitment to the disciple needs to reflect the disciple's level of commitment.

As a disciple builder, realize that disciples do not all grow at the same rate. Based on emotional maturity, personality and personal circumstances, growth rates will vary. Learn to be comfortable with (and sensitive to) the fact that growth in an individual, and therefore in a group, will not be orderly nor perfectly predictable. Guidelines presented here are just that – guidelines, not rigid standards.

You know that a disciple is becoming a "Ministry Trainee" (Phase III: Equipping for Ministry) when he exhibits the traits and habits listed in "A" (Accountability) consistently. These are evidence of a strong personal relationship with Christ, which is the critical foundational need at this point. To hurry the development of this relationship is a mistake. Remember that Christlike character as well as conduct is the goal – not just doing the right things, but being a "virtuous" person and turning away from sin as a lifestyle.

Understanding and Growth (P) Disciple Builder prays:

14a   For disciple to understand who Jesus is, what He has done and how to walk with Him, and to begin to meet with Christ in a daily quiet time (John 6:44; Ephesians 1:18-22).

14b   For personal needs in disciple's life, for disciple's growth in dependence on Jesus to meet personal needs, to see Jesus work in day-to-day life.

14c   For disciple to continue to turn from old lifestyle, establish new habits, experience Christian fellowship, develop a seriousness about God's will and Word.

14d   For disciple to develop healthy ways of dealing with emotions and getting needs met.

Involvement in Body of Christ (S) Disciple:

15a   Is allowed to observe leader in relationship with God and in ministry situations; disciple meets with leader periodically.

15b   Is asked to help with tasks (especially physical tasks, not tasks that require spiritual experience and maturity). Is asked to get involved in the body of Christ.

15c   Attends small group Bible study and/or a *Restoring Your Heart* group (if applicable).

Phase III: Equipping for Ministry

Mentoring (R) Disciple Builder:

16a   Chooses a select, open group of disciples. New people may be added, but group membership is by invitation only. Group is used as a filtering process to determine who should be appointed leaders later.

16b   Meets regularly with the disciple to apply basic ministry skill material (especially "P"—Participation of OPSI), to develop a good personal relationship and to hold each other accountable for personal and spiritual goals.

16c   Encourages disciple to establish casual friendships with unbelievers and to grow in commitment to other believers (in social situations, service activities, projects, etc.).

16d   Encourages disciple to learn relational principles and skills.

Law and Grace (C) Disciple Builder:

17a   Trains disciple in basic ministry skills: evangelism, testimony preparation, inductive Bible study, time management and healthy relationships.

17b   Teaches disciple about nature of God's Kingdom: benefits of Christ's redemptive work (deliverance from disease, demons and death, forgiveness of sin, justification by faith and freedom from the law), the power and leadership of Holy Spirit, spiritual warfare and walking by grace (not under law).

17c   Teaches disciple the vision of discipleship. Emphasizes balance between evangelism and service, adapting the Gospel, and the priority of ministry (balance).

17d   Teaches disciple how to develop healthy relationships.

Disciple Builder: Remember that the truth Christ taught His disciples often unfolded in stages throughout the growth process. This is true in the area of spiritual warfare. At the Ministry Trainee level (Phase III: Equipping for Ministry), you need to focus on the fact that there are opposing forces in our world, the sources of those forces, the supremacy of Christ in the warfare and the weapons of warfare believers have.

Becomes Ministry-Minded (A) Disciple:

18a   Begins to minister to those around him: takes responsibility for tasks within the ministry ("P"—Participation—part of OPSI) and shares Christ with others (including testimony and follow-up).

18b   Actively takes a stand for the Gospel by sharing his faith and by being identified with Christians.

18c   Makes ministry a priority: develops Christian friends to minister with, is accountable to leader (ministry trainer), is a faithful member of group designed to teach ministry skills and develops a vision for discipleship.

18d   Develops healthy relationships and proper boundaries in ministry endeavors.

Disciple Builder: Part of the purpose of taking responsibility for tasks within the ministry is to give the disciple an opportunity to try different areas of ministry to discover his spiritual gifts. The phrase "being identified with Christians" in 18b does not refer to the fact that a disciple needs to be publicly identified with Christ through baptism. (Ideally, this faith step already was taken when the disciple became a Christian.) It does refer to the disciple actively taking a stand for the Gospel by sharing his faith, giving a personal testimony, being identified with a Christian ministry, etc.

When a disciple understands how to develop

healthy relationships, he does not force the Gospel on others and does not try to manipulate a response to the Gospel. He also knows how to maintain healthy boundaries in ministry so he doesn't allow others to take advantage of his time and resources.

When a disciple exhibits the elements listed above in "A" (Accountability), he is showing evidence of being ready to be appointed as a "New Leader" (Phase IV: Developing New Leaders). As before, remember that growth is more than just doing activities. In addition to doing the right activities, there needs to be growth in godly character. In this Phase, there is an emphasis on having a correct assessment of and perspective on the spiritual world.

Courage and Provision (P) Disciple Builder prays:

19a   That disciple sees the priority of ministry, grows in desire for ministry, and has opportunities to minister and grow in commitment to the body (Luke 5:8-10).

19b   That disciple understands Jesus' power to forgive (Luke 5:16-26).

19c   That there will be an open door for Gospel, that disciple will develop a burden for the lost and become bold in his witness.

19d   That disciple understands that having healthy relationships is a priority if he is to be effective in ministry.

Opportunity to Serve and Witness (S) Disciple:

20a   Accepts small challenges in ministry (Does "P"—Participation—part of OPSI).

20b   Is in a Ministry Training group.

20c   Attends a short-term mission project.

20d   Learns about ministry relationships from a variety of ministry opportunities.

Phase IV: Developing New Leaders

Part A — Appointing New Leaders

Training (R) Disciple Builder:

21a   Chooses select, closed group of disciples (for leadership group).

21b   Encourages strong commitments among this group of disciples.

21c   Meets regularly with disciple and continues to be a model for him.

Disciple Builder: Choosing leaders is a critical event in the life of a group as well as in the lives of disciples. Be sure to apply biblical qualifications — especially godly character — as you evaluate (qualities in the Sermon on the Mount). Jesus spent all night in prayer before choosing the Twelve. Thus, we need to follow His example and seek God diligently and humbly when choosing leaders.

There are some common mistakes to avoid when appointing leaders. First, do not appoint people as leaders before they have had enough time and opportunity to demonstrate faithfulness. The leader needs to observe and interact with the disciple over time. On the other hand, do not wait too long to give developing leaders responsibilities. We all grow by being challenged! Obviously, a balance is needed: prayer and careful discernment are necessary. Also, if there are no people to lead, do not appoint leaders.

Leadership Principles: Character, Authority (C) Disciple Builder:

22a   Teaches Sermon on the Mount. Includes topics such as Christian character, ethical conduct, meaning of heart obedience, true worship, eternal perspective on issues in culture, and parables of the Kingdom (Matthew 13).

22b   Teaches Parables of the Kingdom including extending the kingdom to others, con-

flict with Satan's kingdom (spiritual warfare), and growth of the Kingdom.

22c   Teaches about discipleship in the family, spiritual gifts, discipleship philosophy (an overview), and ministry to the hurting (healing).

Disciple Builder: The concept of the "Kingdom" and believers as "Kingdom people" is a theme at this point and should be emphasized. Disciples should be encouraged to try different ministry situations with the goal of discovering their spiritual gifts. New leaders should be learning to identify emotional problems and how to help others begin to heal.

Assumes Leadership Responsibilities (A) Disciple:

23a   Has a personal ministry ("S"—Supervision—of OPSI): assumes responsibility and leadership in ministry, grows in his ability to study the Bible (inductive Bible study and special literature like Parables), and faithfully shares the Gospel.

23b   Has a consistent walk with God, exhibits godly character (Sermon on the Mount) and grows in dependence on God.

23c   Takes bold stands on spiritual and moral issues.

Disciple Builder: Realize that your disciple, a new leader, has needs and areas to continue to grow in and does not have experience to draw from. Therefore you may need to drop back to the "P" phase of OPSI in an area to meet a need he has. When a disciple exhibits the elements listed above in "A" (Accountability), he is showing evidence of being ready to move on to the stage of Phase IV: Developing New Leaders – Part B. Again, the emphasis is not on living the Christian life perfectly, but on general growth progressing toward Christlike maturity.

Perspective and Wisdom (P) Disciple Builder prays:

24a   For discernment in selection of new leaders.

24b   For disciples (new leaders) to have an effective ministry to others. Prays that there are new disciples for new leaders to lead, that disciples are able to see potential in younger believers, and that disciples are strengthened by the Holy Spirit.

24c   For disciples to continue to grow in godly character, to be obedient to the principles in Sermon on Mount, and to be protected from the evil one (especially from spiritual pride).

Appointment to Leadership Roles (S) Disciple:

25a   Participates in leadership group (retreats, meetings, etc.) and in mission projects (short-term, domestic and overseas).

25b   Meets regularly with leader for accountability, encouragement and instruction.

25c   Has a personal ministry ("S"—Supervision—of OPSI) and provides leadership in the movement.

Part B — Focusing on Eternal Things

Encouraging (R) Disciple Builder:

26a   Continues with select, closed group chosen in Phase IV-A, and builds intimate relationships.

26b   Models transparency.

26c   Makes sure that disciple has a personal ministry with believers being equipped for ministry ("S"—Supervision— of OPSI).

Eternal Perspective (C) Disciple Builder:

27a   Teaches disciples to re-evaluate their world view: eternal values are superior to temporal ones (Philippians 1:12-14,18). This includes racial and cross-cultural issues, materialism, legalism, etc.

27b   Teaches about Christ's sufficiency: His provision enables us to do whatever He demands. Victory in spiritual battle comes only by the Holy Spirit.

27c   Teaches about sovereignty of God: how to follow divine authority over human tradition, about biblical authority and how it should be administered, and about the openness of the kingdom to all (universal nature of the church).

27d   Teaches about having realistic biblical expectations for Christian growth and development. Teaches about how to "sort out good and bad." (That is, teaches disciple how to emotionally live with the simultaneous existence of good and bad in himself, in others and in our world.)

Disciple Builder: The theme of "eternal vs. temporal" values affects many areas of a disciple's life in addition to the ones listed in 27a. The general principle is that daily life is filled with choices – how to spend money, where to live, where to work, etc. – and eternal values need to be the guide for decision-making rather that temporal ones.

Regarding 27d: included here is a theology of suffering. How does a Christian deal with hard times, illnesses, disappointments, failure, etc.? Too often, Christian culture does not address these issues, and thus seems to imply that they do not exist for the Christian. A related issue is the fact that as Christians we live in a state of "now but not yet" – the kingdom has come on earth through and in us, and yet, at the same time, the kingdom is still in the future.

Adjusts Expectations (A) Disciple:

28a   Rejects worldly values and embraces eternal values.

28b   Submits to biblical authorities and to Word of God (over the word of men).

28c   Lives in a way that reflects God's grace and obedience rather than a rewards/punishment mind-set.

28d   Has realistic view of the world and himself as being both good and bad. Is able to give himself and others grace.

Disciple Builder: When a disciple exhibits the elements listed above in "A" (Accountability), he is showing evidence of being ready to move on to the stage of Phase V: Developing Mature Leaders – Part A. The disciple continues to have a ministry.

Endurance (P) Disciple Builder prays:

29a   That disciple will be discerning and live for eternal values.

29b   That disciple will see the glorified Christ – His authority on earth and in heaven.

29c   That disciple will have understanding in spiritual battles.

29d   That disciple has an accurate view of God, self and others.

Acceptance of Difficult Assignments (S) Disciple:

30a   Participates in leadership group (retreats, meetings, etc.) and in mission projects (short-term, domestic and overseas).

30b   Meets regularly with the leader for accountability, encouragement and instruction.

30c   Participates in evangelistic outreaches to new classes of people.

Disciple Builder: It is important that content in this section be taught in an atmosphere of grace and encouragement. Many of the topics deal with principles of lifestyle (how much is enough, living a simple life, etc.), and an improper emphasis on these topics can develop. Some people tend to drift toward the extreme of asceticism in which there is a belief that it is "more spiritual" to do without and to judge people who don't agree. Be sensitive to this danger.

Phase V: Developing Mature Leaders

Part A—Delegating New Responsibilities

Delegating (R) Disciple Builder:

31a   Continues with select, closed group chosen in Phase IV-A, and continues to build intimate relationships.

31b   Models suffering love to disciples (leadership team).

31c   Also, models loyalty and faithfulness to disciples (leadership team).

Team Ministry (C) Disciple Builder:

32a   Models and teaches: unity and harmony in the body of Christ; discipline in the body of Christ; reconciliation of brother in sin; and trust in Christ to work in other members of the body (Romans 14).

32b   Models and teaches how to deal with conflicts outside the body regarding false religions and opposition from Christians outside the group.

32c   Teaches team leadership and delegation of responsibility, and develops ministries related to spiritual gifts and calling.

Fosters Unity (A) Disciple:

33a   Willingly forgives an offending brother.

33b   Trusts God to work through others in the midst of disagreements.

33c   Submits to difficult authorities without compromising truth.

33d   Helps give leadership to the overall ministry and to a specialized ministry related to gifting.

Disciple Builder: When disciples exhibit the elements listed above in "A" (Accountability), they are showing evidence of being ready to move on to the stage of Phase V: Developing Mature Leaders – Part B. Other qualities that will be evident are an ability to delegate (trust God to work in and through others), to confront sin and to grow in unselfishness.

Unity in Diversity (P) Disciple Builder prays:

34a   That disciple will have a burden for intercessory prayer.

34b   That disciple will deal with confrontation in the body in a biblical way (Matthew 18:15-21).

34c   That disciple will be bold and be protected from Satan's attacks and criticism.

34d   That disciple will remain humble and learn to serve those he is leading.

Ability to Work with Other Leaders (S) Disciple:

35a   Participates in the leadership group (retreats, meetings, etc.).

35b   Meets regularly with the leader for accountability, encouragement and instruction.

35c   Provides leadership in the overall movement.

Disciple Builder: A pitfall at this point is to fail to give the mature leader increasing responsibility and decision-making authority. A disciple needs to be operating relatively independently in his ministry with occasional check-in points for accountability and advice. In contrast, the personal relationship with the disciple deepens and grows in commitment.

Part B—Casting a World Vision

Commissioning (R) Disciple Builder:

36a   Continues with select, closed group. Helps them build intimate relationships. Has disciples participate on a leadership team.

36b   Is sure that disciple's relationship with him is primarily a peer relationship.

36c   Perseveres in difficult relationships.

Resurrection Power in Daily Life (C)
Disciple Builder:

37a   Teaches all-sufficiency of Christ as He ministered and rested in the power of the Spirit rather than in the flesh. Also teaches about spiritual warfare and dependent prayer.

37b   Teaches and models sacrificial nature of leadership: throne perspective (i.e., all things are ours, so give up the world) and love, as the mark of the Christian.

37c   Teaches about developing a world vision and about personal responsibility to spread the gospel.

Disciple Builder: You as the leader may need to help the disciple articulate specific goals for ministry.

Show Sacrificial Love to Reach the World (A)
Disciple:

38a   Trusts and rests in the Spirit alone in spite of circumstances. Consistently desires to show suffering love.

38b   Lives life characterized by dependent prayer.

38c   Has a ministry vision and a world vision.

Disciple Builder: It is important to help the disciple avoid the danger of self-confident professionalism, i.e., trusting abilities, especially ministry abilities, instead of God.

Sacrificial Love (P) Disciple Builder
prays:

39a   That disciple understands that ministry can be carried out only in the power of the Holy Spirit.

39b   That Holy Spirit works in lives as Gospel is proclaimed.

39c   That disciple and his ministry are protected from power of Satan.

Acceptance of Worldwide Challenge (S)
Disciple:

40a   Takes leadership in the movement.

40b   Functions independently from leader.

40c   Attends and/or organizes prayer meetings for empowering disciples to be Christ's witnesses.

Exhibit C:

Christian Growth Checklist

The *Christian Growth Checklist (CGC)* is available at
http://www.disciplebuilding.org/store

We believe that materials such as these are always "in process" and able to be improved. We will be grateful to receive any feedback you have to share with us. Please send any comments and/or suggestions to:

Worldwide Discipleship Association

(Attention: Margaret Garner)

P.O. Box 142437

Fayetteville, GA 30214

E-mail: mgarner@disciplebuilding.org

Scripture quotations, unless otherwise indicated are from the New International Version of the Bible, © 1978 by New York International Bible Society.

NOTE: In the interest of editorial brevity and simplicity, these documents treat gender-neutral and gender- plural references with the masculine pronoun "he" rather than "she," "he or she" or other constructions. When clarity is better served by other words, we follow whatever usage seems to aid readers best. Worldwide Discipleship Association follows Scripture in joyfully recognizing that God created man and woman in His image as equal recipients of His grace and mercy.

Christian Growth Checklist

Development and Writing Team:

Margaret Garner

Jack Larson

Dr. Joyce Webb

Christian Growth Checklist (CGC)

Worldwide Discipleship Association

"A student…who is fully taught will be like his teacher."—Luke 6:40
"And Jesus grew in wisdom and stature, and in favor with God and men."—Luke 2:52

One of the most important activities of a disciple builder in the disciple building process is discerning the needs of his disciple and then setting goals and designing plans based on those needs. Knowing this, we saw the need for an instrument that helps a mentor (disciple builder) and the disciple systematically evaluate where the disciple is in his development of 1) biblical knowledge and ministry skills (equipping) and 2) emotional health and relational skills (restoring).

The goal is NOT to "test" the disciple with the purpose of rewards or punishment, but the goal IS to give the disciple and his mentor clear information about what content, skills, and abilities (both in equipping areas and in restorative areas) the disciple has and what he still needs to learn and develop within the progressive disciple building model.

This instrument is divided into two parts. Part A addresses Equipping Areas of need. Part B deals with the areas of emotional and relational need—Restorative Areas. At the beginning of each part you will find comments and instructions.

For a complete discussion about planning growth projects for disciples based on the results of the *Christian Growth Checklist*, refer to *Disciple Building: A Practical Strategy*, available from WDA. Visit our website at www.disciplebuilding.org to download samples and order *A Practical Strategy* and other materials. To order additional copies of the *Christian Growth Checklist* see our website.

CHECKLIST A:
Equipping Areas

This checklist tracks the degree to which a disciple has been equipped or trained in his ministry and leadership development. It focuses particularly on the knowledge and skills (**wisdom**) he has gained concerning God and His Kingdom, and measures the roles and responsibilities (**stature**) he has assumed in furthering God's kingdom.

Some of the items on the list are concerned with **concepts that we know**. Other items deal more with **activities that are part of our lives.** In some cases there may be some overlap or degrees of application. We encourage you to check items only when you have achieved a fair degree of consistency in that activity and when your knowledge has resulted in a sense of assurance and confidence.

The Checklist will:

- **Help you discover any "holes" in your development.** You will be able to identify specific areas that need attention from a previous phase(s).

- **It will help you target areas you need to focus on as you continue to grow.** By looking ahead to other areas of growth, you can anticipate the specific skills and concepts you will want to consider, and begin to design strategies to address these.

How to use this Checklist:

- You may use this Checklist to get general information about where you are in the spiritual growth process. The Phase of growth at which you have checked most, if not all, items suggests your level of spiritual maturity. For more information about the phases of growth see *Disciple Building: A Biblical Framework.*

- You may choose to use this Checklist **as a tool to help you develop a personal growth project**, either for yourself or for a disciple. To develop a personal growth project, you will need to take the results of this Checklist, prioritize the areas of need and write goals and projects designed to meet the needs.

  When you come to a Phase in the Checklist in which you mark one-half or fewer of the items, this indicates that you need training and growth at this phase, and possibly, at the previous phase. While most people will have a few items checked in each of the phases, the target phase for planning a growth project is the highest phase with a predominance of checked items.

  Begin your planning by "filling in the holes" from this phase (the items not checked). From there, go to items at the next Phase. Prioritizing these areas of need is essential. Writing goals and projects comes after the prioritizing. (See *Life Coaching Manual*, WDA.)

- Another effective use of this *Checklist* is for a disciple **to ask a mentor and/or close friend for feedback by having them complete the** *Checklist* **on him**. This can provide an excellent opportunity for communication about possible blind spots.

Remember, this is for your benefit. There are *no "right" or "wrong" answers,* merely indications of where you are on a growth continuum. This indicates your personal maturity level, and this knowledge should be a cause for both celebration and motivation. You should celebrate that God has brought you so far in your faith and that you have responded to His leadership. It should also motivate you to continue to grow. Therefore, it is to your advantage to be consistent and honest in your appraisal of yourself. No one will see your checklist except you and those you choose to share the information with.

This is not a test. It is an indicator of where you are in your Christian growth so that you and/or your mentor (disciple builder) can plan the best strategy for your development.

The concepts that form the foundation for the items on this list are derived from Christ's teaching and from a historical orthodox view of Scripture. It is designed primarily to help mark milestones on our spiritual journey. It is not intended to be a position for launching theological teaching or debate.

Instructions

Read over the items in each Phase and mark the items that are true of you. Continue marking items in each Phase until you come to a Phase in which you mark fewer than one-half of the items. This indicates that you need training and growth at this phase, and possibly, at the previous phase.

Remember, try to be consistent and honest in your appraisal of yourself. Celebrate what God has done in your life and eagerly anticipate what He will do!

Phase I-B: Follow Up

1. ❑ I understand that God loves me.

2. ❑ I have admitted that I have a problem with sin and need a savior.

3. ❑ I know that my sin caused a separation between God and me before I became a Christian.

4. ❑ I know that my good deeds are not the basis of my salvation.

5. ❑ I know that if unbelievers continue to reject Christ they will experience separation from God and eternal damnation.

6. ❑ I know that I am forgiven because Christ died on the cross to pay the penalty for my sin.

7. ❑ I know that Jesus Christ is the only way that people can be brought into a relationship with God.

8. ❑ I know that the Bible is the Word of God.

9. ❑ I know that I have eternal life.

10. ❑ I have acknowledged my faith in Jesus Christ through baptism.

11. ❑ I have placed my faith in Christ alone for salvation.

12. ❑ I realize that the Christian life is a journey that will last a lifetime.

13. ❑ I have a desire to follow Christ.

14. ❑ I find myself trusting Christ in new ways.

15. ❑ My care and concern for others has increased.

Phase II: Laying Foundations

16. ❑ I know that I am a new person now that I have trusted Jesus Christ.

17. ❑ I know that the Holy Spirit lives in me and will empower me to live the Christian life.

18. ❑ I know how to be filled with the Spirit.

19. ❑ I know that Jesus Christ is coming again.

20. ❑ I have seen God answer specific prayers related to my everyday needs.

21. ❑ I have experienced God's guidance and direction about a particular matter.

22. ❑ I regularly attend a local church.

23. ❑ I am learning to understand and apply the Bible to my daily life.

24. ❑ I am establishing a personal devotional time in my daily routine.

25. ❑ Since becoming a Christian, I have sinned and have experienced both the discipline and forgiveness of God.

26. ❑ I am in a small group that meets regularly for Bible study and encouragement.

27. ❑ I know that God is a just, benevolent, all-powerful Father.

28. ❏ I know that God has a three-in-one nature: Father, Son, and Holy Spirit.

29. ❏ I understand Jesus to be God, reigning in heaven.

30. ❏ I have an increasing interest in telling others about Jesus.

31. ❏ I'm developing a day-to-day walk with the living Christ.

Phase III: Equipping For Ministry

32. ❏ I know how to explain to someone else how to become a Christian.

33. ❏ I know how to lead an evangelistic Bible study.

34. ❏ I have participated in an organized evangelistic outreach.

35. ❏ I have shared my Christian testimony with a non-Christian.

36. ❏ I have shared the Gospel with a non-Christian.

37. ❏ I regularly contribute a portion of my income to God's work.

38. ❏ I am beginning to discover my unique abilities and contributions to God's kingdom by participating in a variety of ministry situations.

39. ❏ I have learned how to study the Scriptures in a simple, but systematic way.

40. ❏ I have established a regular daily time to read the Bible and pray.

41. ❏ I have seen God's supernatural provision to meet needs.

42. ❏ I have been part of a group that learned how to minister to the needs of others.

43. ❏ I have let people in my daily world know that I am a Christian.

44. ❏ I have taken a new Christian through basic follow-up.

45. ❏ I am aware that there is spiritual warfare going on around me.

46. ❏ I am aware of a situation in which Christ's power has overcome evil.

47. ❏ I believe that Jesus defeated Satan at the cross.

48. ❏ I am deeply concerned about people dying without knowing Christ.

49. ❏ I meet regularly with an older Christian for the purpose of being trained and encouraged.

50. ❏ I know a biblical defense of who Jesus is and His role in salvation.

51. ❏ I have experienced power from the Holy Spirit in a witnessing situation.

52. ❏ I understand that God has declared me righteous in Christ.

53. ❏ I know that Jesus' death on the Cross satisfied God's wrath toward my sin and removed all hostility between us.

54. ❏ I understand that my acceptance by God is based only on what Christ has done for me and never on my works.

55. ❏ I understand that what is true of Christ in His humanity is true of Christians through our union with Christ.

56. ❏ I have learned to answer the most common questions non-believers ask.

57. ❏ I have had to adjust my schedule in order to make ministry to others a priority.

58. ❏ I am beginning to see through my ministry experience that I am a part of God's larger plan to impact the world.

59. ❏ I've come to understand that although God

calls believers to share the gospel with others, no one comes to Christ unless God draws him.

60. ❏ I have at least three non-believers that I pray for regularly.

Phase IV-A: Appointing New Leaders

61. ❏ I can remember several occasions when I had to say "no" to something I wanted to do in order to minister to others.

62. ❏ I am able to write down the character qualities that Jesus presented in the Sermon on the Mount and expects His disciples to exhibit.

63. ❏ I know the biblical teaching on spiritual gifts.

64. ❏ I know how to study a specific book of Scripture.

65. ❏ I know how to study a specific topic in Scripture.

66. ❏ I know the principles of biblical interpretation.

67. ❏ I know how to prepare a small group Bible study lesson.

68. ❏ I have received training in small group leadership.

69. ❏ I can write down at least 3 principles of spiritual warfare.

70. ❏ I have been a key player in a spiritual warfare situation in which there was an obvious change for the good.

71. ❏ I have helped a believer establish a personal devotional time.

72. ❏ I can remember at least three times in the past year when I initiated sharing the Gospel with people I did not know.

73. ❏ I am accountable to a more mature Christian with whom I meet regularly.

74. ❏ I have accepted responsibility for the spiritual development of others by leading a small discipleship group.

75. ❏ I have received positive feedback about my leadership of a small group.

76. ❏ I have confronted another Christian about an area of sin in his life.

77. ❏ I am able to recognize and avoid getting caught up in legalism.

78. ❏ I have devoted myself to a team that is providing leadership to a group of young believers.

79. ❏ I am able to discuss spiritual matters in a loving respectful manner with people who are hostile toward the Gospel.

80. ❏ I have a systematic plan for praying for disciples under my care.

81. ❏ I have grown to the point that I can receive correction from another person.

Phase IV-B: Focusing on Eternal Things

82. ❏ I know how to recognize the errors of non-Christian cults and religions.

83. ❏ I have endured a difficult test that made me less concerned about matters here and now and more concerned about eternal things.

84. ❏ I am part of a group of leaders that is responsible for a specific, ongoing ministry in a church or a Christian organization.

85. ❏ It is becoming clearer to me what my strengths and spiritual gifts are.

86. ❏ I have trained others how to carry out evangelism.

87. ❏ I know how to help other believers study the Bible.

88. ❏ I have ministered in a culture other than my own.

89. ❑ I have come to see that it is easy to do things that look spiritual yet do not reflect true spirituality.

90. ❑ I can remember a time in the past year when I did not understand what God was doing but was able to continue to walk with Him and trust Him in spite of it.

91. ❑ I have been in a situation where it was very unpopular to voice or live the biblical convictions I hold.

92. ❑ In at least one situation this past year, I realized that my expectations of the Christian life were unrealistic, and I had to rethink and adjust them.

93. ❑ In the past year I trusted Christ for something I never thought I could.

94. ❑ I've come to understand that suffering plays a positive, important role in the Christian life.

95. ❑ I have gone through some difficult experiences this year that have convinced me that Jesus is the only one I can trust.

96. ❑ I know that my tendency to sin will not go away as long as I am alive on this earth.

97. ❑ I have asked God to help me make eternal things a priority.

Phase V-A: Delegating New Responsibilities

98. ❑ I'm able to trust God to work in and through other Christians He has placed in my life, even when I disagree with them.

99. ❑ I know how to interpret and teach the Scriptures.

100. ❑ I am able to deflect gossip and deal with slander.

101. ❑ I am able to help Christians work through conflicts.

102. ❑ I know how to recognize those who struggle with emotional problems and help them or assist them in finding help.

103. ❑ My ministry is being formed more and more around my strengths and spiritual gifts.

104. ❑ I am part of a leadership team that arrives at unity by making decisions by consensus.

105. ❑ I have wrestled with the biblical teaching about the miraculous gifts of the Spirit and their place in the church.

106. ❑ I have an organized, systematic prayer strategy.

107. ❑ I have studied the purpose of the church and how it is suppose to function, both internally and toward the world.

108. ❑ I am making progress in an area of my life in which I previously habitually sinned.

109. ❑ I have seen God answer specific requests after I have persevered in prayer.

110. ❑ I have been able to forgive a Christian who has deeply hurt me.

111. ❑ I have been in a situation where I willingly submitted to an authority I did not agree with in a church or Christian organization.

112. ❑ I have endured in a relationship that required me to keep loving and believing the best about a person who was treating me badly.

113. ❑ I am part of a team that makes decisions for a local church or ministry.

114. ❑ I have thought through the biblical teaching about the relationship between Christianity and human government.

115. ❑ I am usually able to appreciate the ministry of other believers without feeling competitive toward them.

116. ❑ I am part of a team that is developing new leaders.

117. ❑ I have been part of the decision-making process when we had to deal with a believer who needed to be subjected to church discipline.

118. ❑ I am learning basic lay-counseling skills.

Phase V-B: Casting A World Vision

119. ❑ I have a vision of how the ministry I have can impact the whole world.

120. ❑ I have given to the Lord's work when I could not afford to.

121. ❑ As I see my own sin and that of the world around me, I find myself longing more and more for Christ's return.

122. ❑ I have a good grasp of the different views on the end times and the return of Christ.

123. ❑ I have an active role (specific prayer, focused giving, being a missionary, corresponding with missionaries, etc.) in reaching other nations with the Gospel.

124. ❑ Younger Christians often come to me seeking guidance about God's will.

125. ❑ Within this past year I went through an experience that humbled me by showing me the seriousness of my sin.

126. ❑ I have endured a time of trouble that taught me not to rely on my own strength and resources, but on Christ.

127. ❑ As my intimacy with God increases, my burden to pray for His church and the world increases.

128. ❑ I can name several areas in my life and ministry that would fail miserably without the specific help of God.

129. ❑ Intense spiritual warfare is a common occurrence in my life and ministry.

130. ❑ I have experienced several different situations that have convinced me that Christ is totally sufficient for everything I need.

131. ❑ I am able to make sacrifices for the Kingdom of God because my citizenship is in heaven.

132. ❑ I count it a privilege to suffer for Christ.

CHECKLIST B:
Restorative Areas

This checklist tracks the degree to which a disciple has developed emotional and relational maturity.

The Checklist will:

- **Help you discover any "holes" in your development.** You will be able to identify specific areas that need attention.

- **It will help you target areas you need to focus on as you continue to grow.** By looking ahead to other areas of growth, you can anticipate the specific skills and concepts you will want to consider, and begin to design strategies to address these.

- Many of the activities and attitudes addressed in this checklist have not been emphasized in Christian discipleship. It is not uncommon for a person to be at an earlier stage of development in this checklist than in the previous checklist (Part A). A healthy goal is for a disciple to be at the same level of maturity in both the equipping and the emotional/relational areas. Thus, attention may need to be given to a weaker area in order to "catch up" with other areas.

How to use this Checklist:

- You may choose to use this Checklist as a tool to help you develop a personal growth project, either for yourself or for a disciple. To develop a personal growth project, you will need to take the results of this Checklist, prioritize the areas of need and write goals and projects designed to meet the needs.

  When you come to a Phase in the Checklist in which you mark one-half or fewer of the items, this indicates that you need training and growth at this phase, and possibly, at the previous phase. While most people will have a few items checked in each of the phases, the target phase for planning a growth project is the highest phase with a predominance of checked items.

  Begin your planning by "filling in the holes" from this phase (the items not checked). From there, go to items at the next Phase. Prioritizing these areas of need is essential. Writing goals and projects comes after the prioritizing. (See *Life Coaching Manual,* WDA.)

- Another effective use of this *Checklist* is for a disciple **to ask a mentor and/or close friend for feedback by having them complete the *Checklist* on him**. This can provide an excellent opportunity for communication about possible blind spots.

Remember, this is for your benefit. There are *no "right" or "wrong" answers,* merely indications of where you are on a growth continuum. This indicates your personal maturity level, and this knowledge should be a cause for both celebration and motivation. You should celebrate that God has brought you so far in your faith and that you have responded to His leadership. It should also motivate you to continue to grow. Therefore, it is to your advantage to be consistent and honest in your appraisal of yourself. No one will see your checklist except you and those you choose to share the information with.

This is not a test. It is an indicator of where you are in your Christian growth so that you and/or your mentor (disciple builder) can plan the best strategy for your development.

The concepts that form the foundation for the items on this list are derived from Christ's teaching and from a historical orthodox view of Scripture. It is designed primarily to help mark milestones on our spiritual journey. It is not intended to be a position for launching theological teaching or debate.

Instructions

Read over the items in each Phase and mark the items that are true of you. Continue marking items in each Phase until you come to a Phase in which you mark fewer than one-half of the items. This indicates that you need training and growth at this phase, and possibly, at the previous phase.

Remember, try to be consistent and honest in your appraisal of yourself. Celebrate what God has done in your life and eagerly anticipate what He will do!

Phase II: Laying Foundations

1. ❑ It is difficult for me to imagine going through life without talking with someone about what's going on with me.

2. ❑ When people share either difficult or good feelings, I am able to experience those feelings with them.

3. ❑ I can count on my family and/or friends when I need sympathy and understanding.

4. ❑ My initial response to an authority is one of co-operation and respect.

5. ❑ If I'm absent from a meeting of my small group, I know I am missed.

6. ❑ I am beginning to understand that God takes note of me as an individual.

7. ❑ Understanding who I am includes knowing I am made in God's image, and yet I am one of a kind.

8. ❑ I am discovering that I can change, and I can choose.

9. ❑ I believe that God created people with needs.

10. ❑ I believe that needs can play a positive role in my life.

11. ❑ I believe that negative emotions can play a positive role in my life.

12. ❑ I know that I am responsible for myself: my needs, emotions, actions, growth.

13. ❑ I understand that although I am greatly influenced by my past, it does not have to determine my future.

14. ❑ I realize that what I think affects how I feel.

15. ❑ I believe giving and/or receiving forgiveness is critical to emotional, relational and spiritual health.

16. ❑ I know of at least one addiction-like behavior that I have struggled with. Examples: food, work, shopping, relationships, TV, computer games, exercise, drugs, perfectionism, sleep, etc.

17. ❑ There are at least two people I could feel comfortable talking with this week about my emotions.

18. ❑ I can list five different emotions I've experienced this past week.

19. ❑ I am usually able to recognize what triggers a particular emotion in myself.

20. ❑ I do not try to avoid feeling certain emotions.

21. ❑ When a person has hurt or angered me, I generally am able to forgive.

22. ❑ In a conflict, I am eventually able to talk to the person I'm angry with in an honest but controlled manner.

23. ❑ I can identify at least three needs for myself (other than physical needs).

24. ❑ I am able to talk with someone I trust about my needs (other than physical needs).

25. ❑ I am willing to allow other people to meet my needs.

26. ❑   After I have sinned and confessed, I'm able to feel forgiven by God fairly soon.

27. ❑   After I have sinned and confessed, I'm able to feel forgiven by myself fairly soon.

28. ❑   I have experienced awe of and appreciation for God.

29. ❑   I enjoy spending time with God.

30. ❑   People who know me well think of me as emotionally stable.

31. ❑   Generally, I feel that God is for me and not against me.

32. ❑   I am able to trust God to provide for my needs.

Phase III: Equipping for Ministry

33. ❑   I am able to bear another's burden without taking responsibility for that person's problem.

34. ❑   Knowing that the only person that can change "me" is "me" keeps me from trying to change others.

35. ❑   When I have a conflict in a relationship I am able to initiate discussion and persist toward a resolution as far as the other person is willing to go.

36. ❑   I can give an example of a time someone had a legitimate need that I could have met, but I knew my limits and was able to say "no."

37. ❑   Others would describe me as a person who "says what he means and means what he says" and does so with tact.

38. ❑   I can recall several people who have told me that they have really felt understood by me.

39. ❑   I can name several people who hold different opinions than I do, but I consider them my friends.

40. ❑   I get a hint of the rejection that Jesus and His followers experienced when I experience rejection and ridicule for my faith.

41. ❑   I am comfortable just being myself instead of pretending to be something I'm not for the sake of belonging.

42. ❑   As I realize that I am truly unique—no one else is like me—I am less likely to compare myself to others to determine my worth.

43. ❑   I can think of a specific ministry project I participated in that showed I can have an impact on others.

44. ❑   I am a person who can initiate and try something new even if it seems risky.

45. ❑   I can name at least one strength and one weakness I have discovered about myself as a result of my participation in ministry.

46. ❑   I realize that I have a responsibility to faithfully minister to others.

47. ❑   I believe I have the power and right to make choices for my life.

48. ❑   I understand that I am not under condemnation for my sin.

49. ❑   I know I can make progress toward experiencing freedom from my old sin pattern.

50. ❑   Within the past month, I can think of at least one instance when I took time for myself even though there were other demands being made of me.

51. ❑   Within the past month, I can think of at least one instance when I chose to delay meeting my own needs in order to meet the needs of others.

52. ❑   When something is legitimately out of my control I am able to let go of it and leave it to God.

53. ❑   realize I cannot change another person even though I can tell him the truth and hold him accountable.

54. ❑   When I am challenged about my belief in the Gospel, I do not compromise.

55. ❑ I consistently tell the truth even when doing so is to my detriment.

56. ❑ I realize that everything I have is a gift from God.

57. ❑ I understand that there is nothing I can do that will cause me to lose God's grace.

58. ❑ I am able to identify fears I have about ministry (e.g. rejection, disappointing others, failure, etc.).

59. ❑ I feel amazed, yet confident, that I'm accepted by God just as I am (with strengths and weaknesses).

60. ❑ I feel increasingly empowered to minister because I'm growing through ministry and relational experiences.

61. ❑ I feel connected with others on an emotional level.

62. ❑ I am able to initiate toward people in ministry because I know they will benefit.

63. ❑ I feel it is acceptable to try and then fail.

Phase IV: Developing New Leaders

64. ❑ I can give an example of a time when I gave my opinion to the leadership team but was able to accept a different decision by the group.

65. ❑ I can explain the negotiation skills I used to reach a compromise in a specific disagreement.

66. ❑ I have experienced being on a leadership team that effectively used problem-solving skills to meet a challenge or resolve a conflict

67. ❑ Someone in leadership would say that I am a person who willingly accepts responsibility to lead as a servant.

68. ❑ As a leader of a small group, I can describe several typical relational problems that I have dealt with successfully.

69. ❑ Although Christ has given me a new heart that wants to please God, I still need to deal with my internal sin nature, which opposes God.

70. ❑ I realize that my problems are not unique—other people struggle with similar problems.

71. ❑ I have discovered my role and potential on a team of leaders.

72. ❑ I am learning to live with the truth and the tension that I am both good and bad.

73. ❑ I am able to write down one spiritual gift I have.

74. ❑ In a sentence I am able to describe a ministry I would love to do (i.e. spend the rest of my life doing).

75. ❑ I know at least one person who would list my strengths and weaknesses the same as I would.

76. ❑ No one has ever told me I am a perfectionist.

77. ❑ No one has ever told me that I live a chaotic life.

78. ❑ Although a few things may be all good or all bad, I usually view most things (situations, people and institutions) as a mixture of good and bad, positive and negative.

79. ❑ Other people tell me that I see things realistically; not making too little or too much of them.

80. ❑ I definitely think things through rather than jumping to conclusions.

81. ❑ People do not accuse me of being overly critical.

82. ❑ I rarely get stuck analyzing, dwelling on, thinking about, one thing.

83. ❑ I typically live in the present rather than getting stuck on the past or worrying about the future.

84. ❑ I'm coming to believe that the problems people have and the solutions needed are more com-

plex than many people think.

85. ❏ I am usually flexible (not too rigid or too legalistic).

86. ❏ I understand that theological truth rarely lies at the extremes but usually is found in the tension between two truths.

87. ❏ On a practical basis, I understand that God has called believers to moderation in most areas of life (e.g. dress, food, finances, etc.).

88. ❏ I feel relieved because I understand that my incompleteness and failure are a normal part of being human.

89. ❏ I feel hopeful and peaceful because I realize that I can survive suffering and that it has positive results.

90. ❏ Because I have accepted the fact that my struggles are a normal part of life, I am able to empathize with others who struggle.

91. ❏ I have experienced greater intimacy with God as a result of suffering.

92. ❏ I have experienced growth in my faith as a result of suffering.

93. ❏ I feel an increased sense of responsibility for the ministry at large.

94. ❏ I feel included as part of a leadership team.

95. ❏ I feel a sense of shared responsibility for the ministry.

Phase V: Developing Mature Leaders

96. ❏ I find from my own personal experience that an effective leadership team requires the participation and cooperation of various people with different gifts.

97. ❏ As a leader, I have participated in mutual accountability within the leadership team and believe it is critical.

98. ❏ I am an integral part of a ministry team that accomplishes amazing things beyond what any of us could do individually.

99. ❏ My personal ministry is an expression of my strengths.

100. ❏ As I have come to understand the importance of eternal matters (e.g. God's sovereignty, His power over evil, the role He gives believers, etc.), it has changed my decisions and priorities.

101. ❏ I have a vision for how the ministry/church/Christian organization that I help give oversight to can change the world.

102. ❏ I have participated in a team that really wrestled to determine God's will.

103. ❏ I feel privileged to be a part of something bigger than myself.

104. ❏ I am determined to defer my preferences to those of the team in order to accomplish more.

105. ❏ I am amazed that God can impact the world through me as a part of a leadership team.

106. ❏ I feel assured of God's sufficiency to supply all we need for the ministry He has given the leadership team.

107. ❏ I am motivated to persevere and sacrifice to accomplish the vision God has given me.

108. ❏ I have a passion for the ministry I am involved in.

NOTE: For assistance in planning growth projects for disciples based on the results of this *Christian Growth Checklist*, refer to *Disciple Building: A Practical Strategy*, available from WDA. Visit our website **www.disciplebuilding.org** to download samples and order *A Practical Strategy* and other materials. To order additional copies of the *Christian Growth Checklist* see our website.

Exhibit D:

Needs Worksheet

NEEDS WORKSHEET
Some Areas to Observe

Physical:
- General health
- Diet
- Rest
- Exercise
- Appearance/grooming
- Special needs
- Financial
- Care of home/possessions

Social:
- Relationship with family
- Relationship with friends (including dating)
- Relationship with Christians
- Relationship with non-Christians
- Time to be alone
- Interaction with people different than themselves

Mental/Intellectual:
- Level of education
- Interest in learning, growing intellectually
- Aptitude for studying/learning
- Study skills
- Understanding/experiencing the world
- Areas of interest/expertise; art, music, literature, applied science, social science

Spiritual:

Private Actions:
- Devotions/service
- Prayer
- Values
- Steps of faith (according to level of maturity)
- Stewardship (money, time, etc.)

Public Actions:
- Identify with Christ/identify with the body of Christ
- Ministry involvement (according to level of maturity)

Spiritual/Emotional: Attitudes/Character/Behavior
- Humble
- Persistent
- Truthful
- Consistent
- Compassionate
- Nervous
- Heart for God
- Hateful
- Teachable
- Vengeful
- Zealous
- Exaggeration
- Patient
- Lying
- Joyful
- Blunt
- Kind
- Gossipy
- Gentle
- Easily embarrassed
- Responsible
- Spirit of excellence
- Prompt
- Distracted
- Defensive
- Self-controlled
- Peaceful
- Diligent
- Anxious
- Jealous
- Complacent
- Loving
- Angry
- Flexible
- Ambitious
- Lustful
- Moody
- Organized
- Depressed
- Takes initiative
- Belligerent
- Content
- Lazy
- Self-motivated
- Fearful
- Immoral
- Guilty
- Pornography
- Discouraged
- Homosexuality
- Faithful
- Argumentative
- Servant-hearted
- Covetous

Exhibit E:

NGP Worksheet

NGP Worksheet

Name:

Date:

Need:
(Remember to prioritize)

Goals:
(Specific and measurable activities that when accomplished will meet the need. Think KABS.)

Projects/Plans:

Relate:

Content:

Accountability:

Pray:

Situations/Structures:

Evaluation:
(How are plans/projects going? Are goals being accomplished? Why/why not? Am I gaining important information? What do I need to do differently?)

Exhibit F:

Mark

- Case Study
  - 2 CGCs
- 4 Sample NGPs

Case Study

Mark is a thirty-five-year-old man who works as a project manager for a computer company. He is married and has two children: six years and three years old.

As a teenager Mark made a commitment to Christ, but was not serious about his relationship with God until a year ago. Since then he has been in a small group Bible study on the book of John and has grown steadily: learning to spend time with the Lord, learning to walk obediently with Christ, and seeing Christ meet his needs. This past year he has worked with the group of men that have the responsibility of keeping up the church building and landscaping.

Recently Mark has begun to be concerned for several of his fellow workers who are not believers and are missing out on a personal relationship with Jesus. He has expressed this concern to some of his Christian friends, but he has also mentioned his sense of inadequacy in sharing with non-Christians.

Mark and his wife, Marsha, have a good relationship. However, at times the many demands of having young children hinder them from maintaining good communication. Also, Mark works long hours. He says that he is committed to spending time with his family, but often allows his work to rob time from them. He and Marsha have had some arguments about his long working hours and neglecting his family.

Mark relates easily to people and has a servant heart. He is known as a loyal friend and at times has trouble saying "no" when his friends ask him to do things for them.

Pages from Mark's Christian Growth Checklist —
Equipping Phase III

Phase II-A: Follow Up

1. ☑ I understand that God loves me.

2. ☑ I have admitted that I have a problem with sin and need a savior.

3. ☑ I know that my sin caused a separation between God and me before I became a Christian.

4. ☑ I know that my good deeds are not the basis of my salvation.

5. ☑ I know that if unbelievers continue to reject Christ they will experience separation from God and eternal damnation.

6. ☑ I know that I am forgiven because Christ died on the cross to pay the penalty for my sin.

7. ☑ I know that Jesus Christ is the only way that people can be brought into a relationship with God.

8. ☑ I know that the Bible is the Word of God.

9. ☑ I know that I have eternal life.

10. ☑ I have acknowledged my faith in Jesus Christ through baptism.

11. ☑ I have placed my faith in Christ alone for salvation.

12. ☑ I realize that the Christian life is a journey that will last a lifetime.

13. ☑ I have a desire to follow Christ.

14. ☑ I find myself trusting Christ in new ways.

15. ☑ My care and concern for others has increased.

Phase II-B: Laying Foundations

16. ☑ I know that I am a new person now that I have trusted Jesus Christ.

17. ☑ I know that the Holy Spirit lives in me and will empower me to live the Christian life.

18. ☑ I know how to be filled with the Spirit.

19. ☑ I know that Jesus Christ is coming again.

20. ☑ I have seen God answer specific prayers related to my everyday needs.

21. ☑ I have experienced God's guidance and direction about a particular matter.

22. ☑ I regularly attend a local church.

23. ☑ I am learning to understand and apply the Bible to my daily life.

24. ☑ I am establishing a personal devotional time in my daily routine.

25. ☑ Since becoming a Christian, I have sinned and have experienced both the discipline and forgiveness of God.

26. ☑ I am in a small group that meets regularly for Bible study and encouragement.

27. ☑ I know that God is a just, benevolent, all-powerful Father.

28. ☑ I know that God has a three-in-one nature: Father, Son, and Holy Spirit.

29. ☑ I understand Jesus to be God, reigning in heaven.

30. ☑ I have an increasing interest in telling others about Jesus.

31. ☑ I'm developing a day-to-day walk with the living Christ.

Phase III: Equipping For Ministry

32. ❏ I know how to explain to someone else how to become a Christian.

33. ❏ I know how to lead an evangelistic Bible study.

34. ❏ I have participated in an organized evangelistic outreach.

35. ❏ I have shared my Christian testimony with a non-Christian.

36. ❏ I have shared the Gospel with a non-Christian.

37. ☑ I regularly contribute a portion of my income to God's work.

38. ❏ I am beginning to discover my unique abilities and contributions to God's kingdom by participating in a variety of ministry situations.

39. ❏ I have learned how to study the Scriptures in a simple, but systematic way.

40. ❏ I have established a regular daily time to read the Bible and pray.

41. ☑ I have seen God's supernatural provision to meet needs.

42. ❏ I have been part of a group that learned how to minister to the needs of others.

43. ❏ I have let people in my daily world know that I am a Christian.

44. ❏ I have taken a new Christian through basic follow-up.

45. ❏ I am aware that there is spiritual warfare going on around me.

46. ❏ I am aware of a situation in which Christ's power has overcome evil.

47. ☑ I believe that Jesus defeated Satan at the cross.

48. ☑ I am deeply concerned about people dying without knowing Christ.

49. ❏ I meet regularly with an older Christian for the purpose of being trained and encouraged.

50. ❏ I know a biblical defense of who Jesus is and His role in salvation.

51. ❏ I have experienced power from the Holy Spirit in a witnessing situation.

52. ❏ I understand that God has declared me righteous in Christ.

53. ☑ I know that Jesus' death on the Cross satisfied God's wrath toward my sin and removed all hostility between us.

54. ☑ I understand that my acceptance by God is based only on what Christ has done for me and never on my works.

55. ❏ I understand that what is true of Christ in His humanity is true of Christians through our union with Christ.

56. ❏ I have learned to answer the most common questions non-believers ask.

57. ❏ I have had to adjust my schedule in order to make ministry to others a priority.

58. ❏ I am beginning to see through my ministry experience that I am a part of God's larger plan to impact the world.

59. ❏ I've come to understand that although God calls believers to share the gospel with others, no one comes to Christ unless God draws him.

60. ❏ I have at least three non-believers that I pray for regularly.

Pages from Mark's Christian Growth Checklist — Restorative Phases II & III

Phase II

1. ☑ It is difficult for me to imagine going through life without talking with someone about what's going on with me.

2. ☑ When people share either difficult or good feelings, I am able to experience those feelings with them.

3. ☑ I can count on my family and/or friends when I need sympathy and understanding.

4. ☑ My initial response to an authority is one of cooperation and respect.

5. ☑ If I'm absent from a meeting of my small group, I know I am missed.

6. ☑ I am beginning to understand that God takes note of me as an individual.

7. ☑ Understanding who I am includes knowing I am made in God's image, and yet I am one of a kind.

8. ☑ I am discovering that I can change, and I can choose.

9. ☐ I believe that God created people with needs.

10. ☐ I believe that needs can play a positive role in my life.

11. ☐ I believe that negative emotions can play a positive role in my life.

12. ☐ I know that I am responsible for myself: my needs, emotions, actions, and growth.

13. ☑ I understand that although I am greatly influenced by my past, it does not have to determine my future.

14. ☑ I realize that what I think affects how I feel.

15. ☑ I believe giving and/or receiving forgiveness is critical to emotional, relational and spiritual health.

16. ☐ I know of at least one addiction like behavior that I have struggled with. Examples: food, work, shopping, relationships, TV, computer games, exercise, drugs, perfectionism, sleep, etc.

17. ☑ There are at least two people I could feel comfortable talking with this week about my emotions.

18. ☐ I can list five different emotions I've experienced this past week.

19. ☐ I am usually able to recognize what triggers a particular emotion in myself.

20. ☐ I do not try to avoid feeling certain emotions.

21. ☑ When a person has hurt or angered me, I generally am able to forgive.

22. ☐ In a conflict, I am eventually able to talk to the person I'm angry with in an honest but controlled manner.

23. ☑ I can identify at least three needs for myself (other than physical needs).

24. ☐ I am able to talk with someone I trust about my needs (other than physical needs).

25. ☑ I am willing to allow other people to meet my needs.

26. ☑ After I have sinned and confessed, I'm able to feel forgiven by God fairly soon.

27. ☑ After I have sinned and confessed, I'm able to feel forgiven by myself fairly soon.

28. ☑ I have experienced awe of and appreciation for God.

29. ☑ I enjoy spending time with God.

30. ☑ People who know me well think of me as emotionally stable.

31. ☑ Generally, I feel that God is for me and not against me.

32. ❏ I am able to trust God to provide for my needs.

Phase III

33. ❏ I am able to bear another's burden without taking responsibility for that person's problem.

34. ☑ Knowing that the only person that can change "me" is "me" keeps me from trying to change others.

35. ❏ When I have a conflict in a relationship I am able to initiate discussion and persist toward a resolution as far as the other person is willing to go.

36. ❏ I can give an example of a time someone had a legitimate need that I could have met, but I knew my limits and was able to say "no."

37. ❏ Others would describe me as a person who "says what he means and means what he says" and does so with tact.

38. ☑ I can recall several people who have told me that they have really felt understood by me.

39. ☑ I can name several people who hold different opinions than I do, but I consider them my friends.

40. ☑ I get a hint of the rejection that Jesus and His followers experienced when I experience rejection and ridicule for my faith.

41. ☑ I am comfortable just being myself instead of pretending to be something I'm not for the sake of belonging.

42. ☑ As I realize that I am truly unique—no one else is like me—I am less likely to compare myself to others to determine my worth.

43. ☑ I can think of a specific ministry project I participated in that showed I can have an impact on others.

44. ☑ I am a person who can initiate and try something new even if it seems risky.

45. ☑ I can name at least one strength and one weakness I have discovered about myself as a result of my participation in ministry.

46. ☑ I realize that I have a responsibility to faithfully minister to others.

47. ☑ I believe I have the power and right to make choices for my life.

48. ☑ I understand that I am not under condemnation for my sin.

49. ☑ I know I can make progress toward experiencing freedom from my old sin pattern.

50. ❏ Within the past month, I can think of at least one instance when I took time for myself even though there were other demands being made of me.

51. ☑ Within the past month, I can think of at least one instance when I chose to delay meeting my own needs in order to meet the needs of others.

52. ☑ When something is legitimately out of my control I am able to let go of it and leave it to God.

53. ❏ I realize I cannot change another person even though I can tell him the truth and hold him accountable.

54. ❏ When I am challenged about my belief in the Gospel, I do not compromise.

55. ☑ I consistently tell the truth even when doing so is to my detriment.

56. ☑ I realize that everything I have is a gift from God.

57. ☑ I understand that there is nothing I can do that will cause me to lose God's grace.

58. ☑ I am able to identify fears I have about ministry (e.g. rejection, disappointing others, failure, etc.).

59. ☑ I feel amazed yet confident that I'm accepted by God just as I am (with strengths and weaknesses).

60. ❏ I feel increasingly empowered to minister because I'm growing through ministry and relational experiences.

61. ❏ I feel connected with others on an emotional level.

62. ❏ I am able to initiate toward people in ministry because I know they will benefit.

63. ☑ I feel it is acceptable to try and then fail.

NGP Worksheet
Sample 1: Phase III—Equipping for Ministry

Name: Mark

Date: September

Need:
(Remember to prioritize)
- To learn to share his faith with others

Goals:
(Specific and measurable activities that when accomplished will meet the need. Think KABS.)
- Attend Campus Crusade evangelism training at First Church on September 9
- Learn to share his testimony
- Share his testimony with 4 people in the next 4 months
- Share the Gospel with at least 4 people in the next 4 months

© 2002–2015 by WDA

Projects/Plans:

Relate:
- Meet with Mark every other Tuesday for breakfast to develop personal relationship and for accountability.
- Do informal activities together several times a month (ex: run errands, work on lawn together, etc.)

Content:
- Basics of sharing the Gospel (content and method)
- "How to Prepare Your Testimony" (WDA)
- List of Mark's friends to pray for regarding their relationship with Christ

Accountability:
- Give Mark brochure and remind him to sign up for and attend Evangelism Training. Attend with him, if possible.
- Ask him how he is doing with respect to applying the Evangelism Training (see Goals #3 and #4). Ask weekly; go out and share with him.

Pray:
- That Mark will: have an increasing burden for the lost, build meaningful relationships with non-Christians, recognize opportunities and boldly share his testimony/the Gospel.

Situations/Structures:
- Campus Crusade Evangelism Training at First Church.
- Outreach Team at church for next 6 months.
- Appointment with me every two weeks.

Evaluation:
(How are plans/projects going? Are goals being accomplished? Why/why not? Am I gaining important information? What do I need to do differently?)

(1 month later)
- Attended evangelism training
- Joined Outreach Team, but missed several weeks because of work schedule. Continues on the Team.
- Faithfully attended the Tuesday morning appointment.
- Has shared testimony with 3 people (2 during outreach and 1 with neighbor). Mark was comfortable doing this and did effectively.
- He has shared the Gospel with 1 person (during outreach). This was more difficult for him than sharing his testimony.
- Realizes that he has missed several opportunities and is frustrated.
- Needs to continue to be encouraged.

NGP Worksheet
Sample 2: Phase III—Equipping for Ministry

Name: Mark

Date: October 18

Need:
(Remember to prioritize)
- To become more consistent in his personal devotional time.

Goals:
(Specific and measurable activities that when accomplished will meet the need. Think KABS.)
- Design a realistic plan for his personal devotional time (when, where, topic, etc.)
- Spend at least 15 minutes a day in personal devotions.
- Be accountable to someone regarding his personal devotional time.

Projects/Plans:

Relate:
- Meet with Mark every other Tuesday for breakfast to develop personal relationship and for accountability.
- Spend informal time together several times a month to build relationship

Content:
- Mark's personal plan for his devotional times.

Accountability:
- Hold Mark accountable for having a plan for his devotions and for spending at least 15 minutes a day with God.

Pray:
- That Mark has a growing desire to meet with God
- That he is wise and discerning regarding spiritual attacks in this area
- That his consistency improves without accompanying legalism or unnecessary pressure

Situations/Structures:
- Appointments every two weeks.

Evaluation:
(How are plans/projects going? Are goals being accomplished? Why/why not? Am I gaining important information? What do I need to do differently?)

(1 month later)
- Faithfully attended Tuesday morning appointment.
- Drew up a plan for his personal devotions
- Mark has a real hunger for spending time with God and is growing in his discipline and time management. A problem seems to be that Mark and his wife often stay up to watch the late show, and then getting up on time is difficult. He is working at getting to bed on time.

© 2002-2015 by WDA

NGP Worksheet
Sample 3: Phase III—Equipping for Ministry

Name: Mark

Date: January 16

Need:
(Remember to prioritize)

- To learn to help a young believer begin to grow spiritually.

Goals:
(Specific and measurable activities that when accomplished will meet the need. Think KABS.)

- Attend 3 teaching sessions re: basic Christian growth

- Accompany me (or another leader) on at least 2 appts. with young believers: a. Personal Devotions, b. Character of God, c. Basic Bible Study Skills

- Establish 1 young believer in the faith (2 if possible).

© 2002-2015 by WDA

Projects/Plans:

Relate:
- Continue to meet with Mark every 2 weeks for personal relationship building, teaching and accountability.

Content:
- Become familiar with WDA's Follow-Up material for a New Believer (Phase I-B). Prepare Mark to present it in either a one-to-one situation or in a small group.

Accountability:
- Use 2 or 3 personal appointments with Mark in February and March to teach the concepts important to a young believer.

- Give Mark homework to be completed before each session.

- Make plans to take him with me on at least 2 appointments I have scheduled with "young believers."

- Hold Mark accountable for homework and appointments.

- Hold him accountable for praying for a new believer to help grow and for wisdom and discernment.

Pray:
- That Mark will have a heart and burden to see young believers grow to maturity, that God will place a young believer in Mark's life for him to help get established in the faith, and that Mark will be wise and discerning as he ministers.

Situations/Structures:
- 3 personal discipleship appointments with discipler.

- Follow up appointments with young believer(s).

Evaluation:
(How are plans/projects going? Are goals being accomplished? Why/why not? Am I gaining important information? What do I need to do differently?)

(2 months later)

- Attended all 3 sessions on follow up material.

- Completed homework assignments.

- Has observed 1 appointment that another leader had with a new believer. A second was scheduled but young believer cancelled. Appointment was rescheduled.

- Has not yet established a young believer in the faith.

NGP Worksheet

Sample 4: Phase III—Equipping for Ministry
Restorative NGP

Name: Mark

Date: September 10

Need:

(Remember to prioritize)

- To "get in touch" with emotions (i.e. better understand and express)

Goals:

(Specific and measurable activities that when accomplished will meet the need. Think KABS.)

- Practice identifying emotions with group/individual
- Practice telling others about his emotions
- Identify specific ways he avoids emotions

Projects/Plans:

Relate:

- Meet with Mark every two weeks to encourage him.
- Challenge him to grow in his ability to understand his needs and emotions.
- Discuss *How Emotional Problems Develop*. Work through *Understanding Emotions Workbook*, if necessary.

Content:

- Have Mark read *How Emotional Problems Develop*.
- Have Mark study *Understanding Emotions Workbook* with restorative group or with me.

Accountability:

- Go through Workbook with Mark (and hold accountable for exercises) or see that he is in a restorative group working through it.

Pray:

- That God will open Mark's eyes to understand why he is out of touch with his emotions.
- That God will help him learn the skills necessary to process his emotions.
- That God will help him get past the fears that prevent him from dealing with his emotions.

Situations/Structures:

- A restorative group (if one is available).
- Personal appointment with me every two weeks

Evaluation:

(How are plans/projects going? Are goals being accomplished? Why/why not? Am I gaining important information? What do I need to do differently?)

(6 months later)

- Is attending a restorative group doing the *Understanding Emotions Workbook*.
- Mark and I meet every two weeks for encouragement and accountability. We will continue to meet.
- Mark can identify and talk about his emotions and is more comfortable with them. He has learned a lot and states that he is "happier."
- His plan is to spend another 6 months in a restorative group working on unresolved pain from his past which surfaced as he worked on his emotions.

Related WDA Resources

Learn More about Life Coaching and Disciple Building

Life Coaching Exhibits/Worksheets (Free)
Get the exhibits and worksheets in printable pdf format
for free from the WDA Store.
http://www.disciplebuilding.org/product-category/life-coaching/
http://www.disciplebuilding.org/store

Life Coaching
See how you can bring Life Coaching to your church and ministry.
http://www.disciplebuilding.org/ministries/church-ministry/life-coaching/

Explore
Watch our WDA video and learn more about us.
http://www.disciplebuilding.org/explore

Maturity Matters

The Priority and Process for Disciple Building in the Church
by Bob Dukes
Get a copy from the WDA Store.
Available in paperback and for Kindle®
http://www.disciplebuilding.org/store